Reading Voyage 3

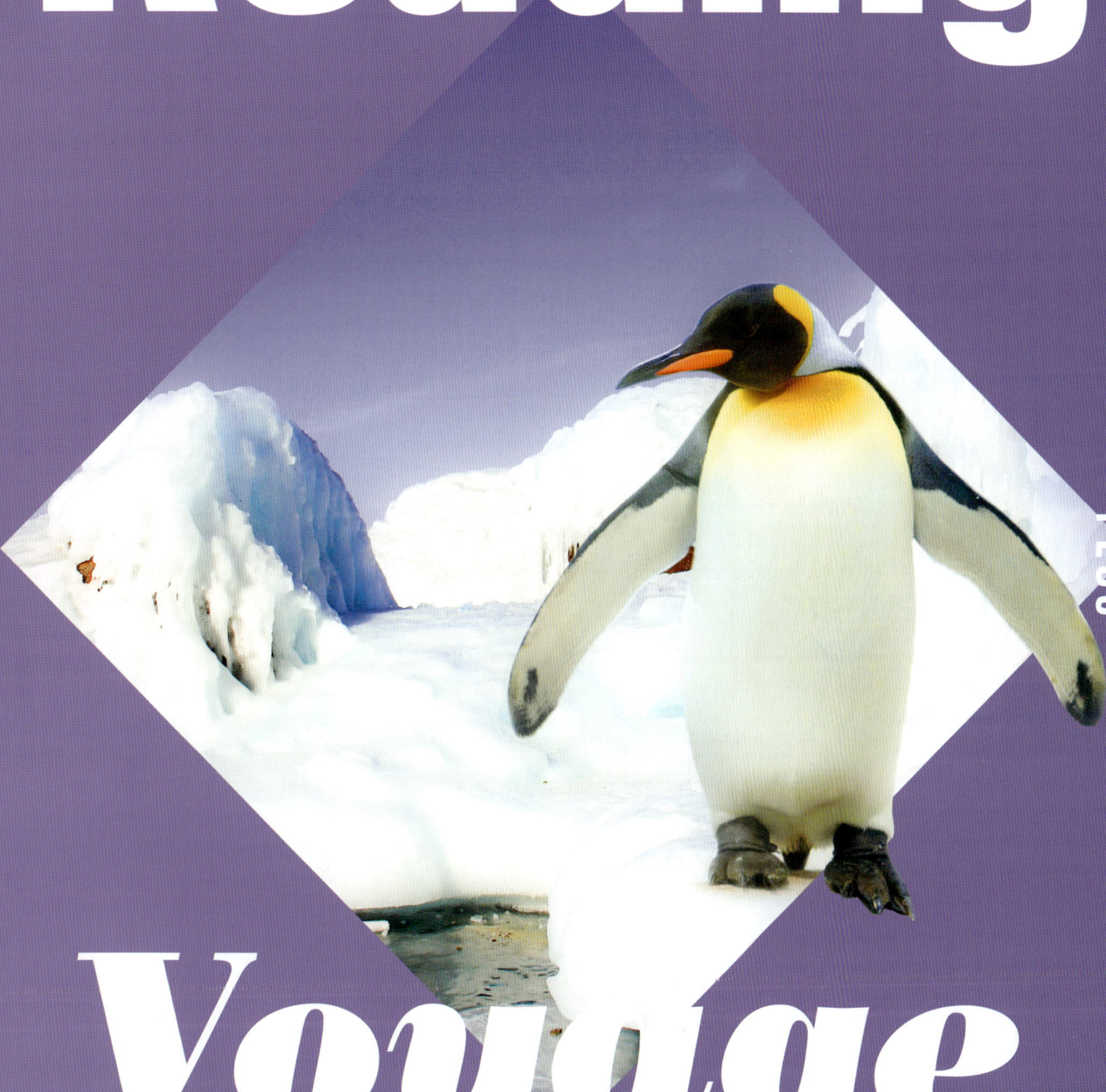

Reading *Voyage*
PLUS 3

Publisher Chung Kyudo
Editors Jeong Yeonsoon, Kim Mina
Authors Jonathan S. McClelland, Neil Armstrong, Shin Yeongju
Proofreaders Michael A. Putlack, Mark Holden
Designer Design Sum

First published in October 2016
By Darakwon, Inc.
Darakwon Bldg., 211, Munbal-ro, Paju-si, Gyeonggi-do 10881
Republic of Korea
Tel: 82-2-736-2031 (Ext. 250)
Fax: 82-2-732-2037

Copyright © 2016 Darakwon, Inc.

All rights reserved. No part of this publication may be reproduced, stored in a retrieval system, or transmitted in any form or by any means, electronic, mechanical, photocopying or otherwise, without the prior consent of the copyright owner. Refund after purchase is possible only according to the company regulations. Contact the above telephone number for any inquiries. Consumer damages caused by loss, damage, etc. can be compensated according to the consumer dispute resolution standards announced by the Korea Fair Trade Commission. An incorrectly collated book will be exchanged.

ISBN 978-89-277-0779-0 58740
      978-89-277-0773-8 58740 (set)

www.darakwon.co.kr

Components Main Book / Workbook
14 13 12 11 10 9 8   25 26 27 28 29

Reading Voyage

PLUS

3

Unit Components

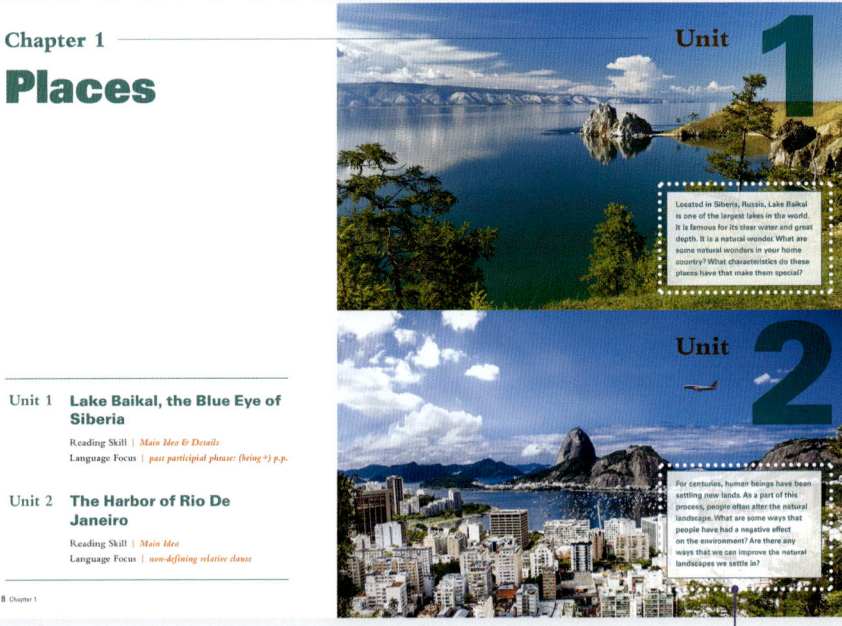

Before You Read

Each chapter consists of two units. Students can read two interesting and informative passages on the same specific theme to gain a broader understanding of the topic.

This section helps students think about and predict the topic by drawing on their background knowledge before reading the passage.

Vocabulary in Context

Students learn the key words from the passage by matching them with their definitions or synonyms in this section.

Main Reading Passage

A focus sentence gives students tips to help them understand the main idea of the text.

The passages are written to be as interesting and informative as possible, covering a variety of topics such as art, history, social issues, etc.

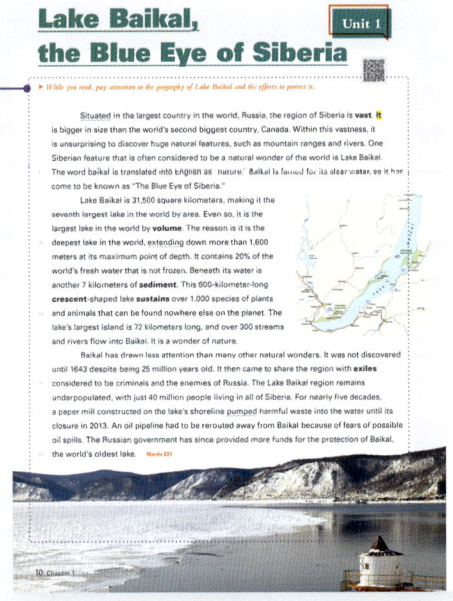

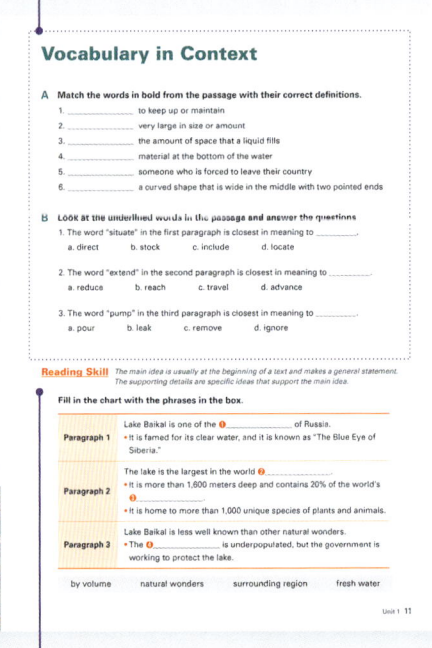

Reading Skill

Students can organize the key concepts of the passage by practicing various reading skills including identifying the main idea, sequencing, cause and effect, and more.

Reading Comprehension

This portion asks students to identify the main idea, details, and draw inferences from the passages through multiple-choice and short-answer questions.

Summary

For the summary, students will review the essential information from the passage.

Language Focus

This section helps students learn key grammar structures from the passage. Students will apply these structures in exercises such as sentence rewriting and choosing the best word form.

Workbook

Extra vocabulary and writing practice, and reading comprehension questions are provided to enable students to review the reading passages more deeply.

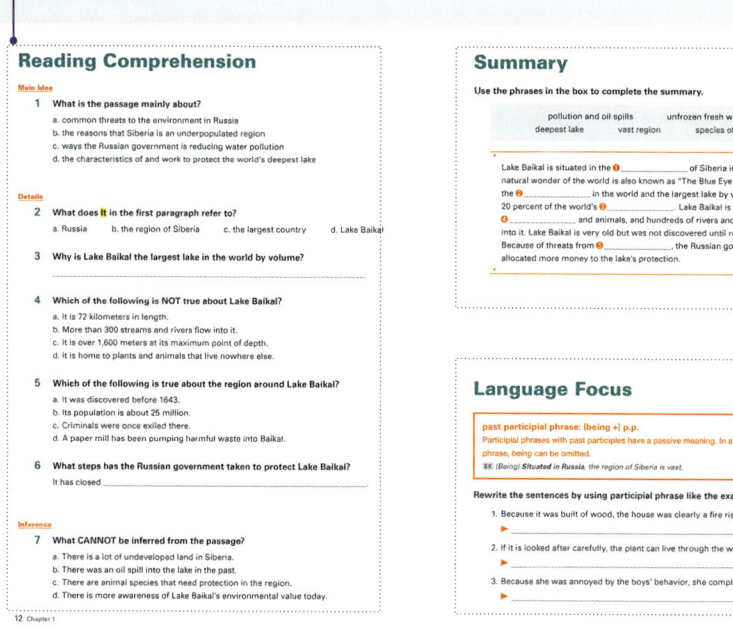

Online Supplement

MP3 files, answer keys, translations, and vocabulary lists are provided free online at www.darakwon.co.kr.

A program for generating vocabulary and writing test sheets is available free online at voca.darakwon.co.kr.

Table of Contents

Chapter	Unit	Title	Reading Skill / Language Focus	Page
1 Places	Unit 1	Lake Baikal, the Blue Eye of Siberia	Main Idea & Details / past participial phrase: (being +) p.p.	8
	Unit 2	The Harbor of Rio De Janeiro	Main Idea / non-defining relative clause	14
2 Social Issues	Unit 3	The Global Refugee Crisis	Main Idea / offer/lend/show + indirect object + direct object	18
	Unit 4	Too Many College Graduates	Cause & Effect / that/those	24
3 Art & People	Unit 5	Andy Warhol, Inventor of Pop Art	Sequencing / perfect participial phrase: having + p.p.	28
	Unit 6	What Is Pop Music?	Main Idea / substitute word *one*	34
4 Food & Environment	Unit 7	Staple Foods Around the World	Main Idea & Details / perfect infinitive: to + have + p.p.	38
	Unit 8	Free-Range Farming	Cause & Effect / be allowed/asked/expected + *to*-infinitive	44

Chapter	Unit	Title	Reading Skill / Language Focus	Page
5 Science	Unit 9	**The Spaceship Cemetery**	Main Idea / much/far/even/a lot + comparatives	48
	Unit 10	**Ancient Chinese and Egyptian Astronomy**	Compare & Contrast / prepositions + which	54
6 Business & Marketing	Unit 11	**Advertising in the Internet Age**	Main Idea / too + adjective/adverb + *to*-infinitive	58
	Unit 12	**Customized Online Ads**	Cause & Effect / the emphatic *do*	64
7 Animals	Unit 13	**Why Can't Ostriches Fly?**	Main Idea & Details / no ~ as + adjective/adverb + as	68
	Unit 14	**The Swimming Nose**	Main Idea / high vs. highly	74
8 History & Origins	Unit 15	**The First Modern Olympics**	Sequencing / It is[was] ~ that	78
	Unit 16	**Calendar Systems of the World**	Categorizing / conjunction (+ subject + be)	84

Chapter 1
Places

Unit 1 Lake Baikal, the Blue Eye of Siberia

Reading Skill | *Main Idea & Details*
Language Focus | *past participial phrase: (being +) p.p.*

Unit 2 The Harbor of Rio De Janeiro

Reading Skill | *Main Idea*
Language Focus | *non-defining relative clause*

Unit 1

Located in Siberia, Russia, Lake Baikal is one of the largest lakes in the world. It is famous for its clear water and great depth. It is a natural wonder. What are some natural wonders in your home country? What characteristics do these places have that make them special?

Unit 2

For centuries, human beings have been settling new lands. As a part of this process, people often alter the natural landscape. What are some ways that people have had a negative effect on the environment? Are there any ways that we can improve the natural landscapes we settle in?

Lake Baikal, the Blue Eye of Siberia

Unit 1

▶ *While you read, pay attention to the geography of Lake Baikal and the efforts to protect it.*

Situated in the largest country in the world, Russia, the region of Siberia is **vast**. It is bigger in size than the world's second biggest country, Canada. Within this vastness, it is unsurprising to discover huge natural features, such as mountain ranges and rivers. One Siberian feature that is often considered to be a natural wonder of the world is Lake Baikal.
5 The word baikal is translated into English as "nature." Baikal is famed for its clear water, so it has come to be known as "The Blue Eye of Siberia."

Lake Baikal is 31,500 square kilometers, making it the seventh largest lake in the world by area. Even so, it is the largest lake in the world by **volume**. The reason is it is the
10 deepest lake in the world, extending down more than 1,600 meters at its maximum point of depth. It contains 20% of the world's fresh water that is not frozen. Beneath its water is another 7 kilometers of **sediment**. This 600-kilometer-long **crescent**-shaped lake **sustains** over 1,000 species of plants
15 and animals that can be found nowhere else on the planet. The lake's largest island is 72 kilometers long, and over 300 streams and rivers flow into Baikal. It is a wonder of nature.

Baikal has drawn less attention than many other natural wonders. It was not discovered until 1643 despite being 25 million years old. It then came to share the region with **exiles**
20 considered to be criminals and the enemies of Russia. The Lake Baikal region remains underpopulated, with just 40 million people living in all of Siberia. For nearly five decades, a paper mill constructed on the lake's shoreline pumped harmful waste into the water until its closure in 2013. An oil pipeline had to be rerouted away from Baikal because of fears of possible oil spills. The Russian government has since provided more funds for the protection of Baikal,
25 the world's oldest lake.   Words 321

Vocabulary in Context

A **Match the words in bold from the passage with their correct definitions.**

1. _____ to keep up or maintain
2. _____ very large in size or amount
3. _____ the amount of space that a liquid fills
4. _____ material at the bottom of the water
5. _____ someone who is forced to leave their country
6. _____ a curved shape that is wide in the middle with two pointed ends

B **Look at the underlined words in the passage and answer the questions.**

1. The word "situate" in the first paragraph is closest in meaning to _____.
   a. direct   b. stock   c. include   d. locate

2. The word "extend" in the second paragraph is closest in meaning to _____.
   a. reduce   b. reach   c. travel   d. advance

3. The word "pump" in the third paragraph is closest in meaning to _____.
   a. pour   b. leak   c. remove   d. ignore

Reading Skill *The main idea is usually at the beginning of a text and makes a general statement. The supporting details are specific ideas that support the main idea.*

Fill in the chart with the phrases in the box.

Paragraph 1	Lake Baikal is one of the ❶_____ of Russia. • It is famed for its clear water, and it is known as "The Blue Eye of Siberia."
Paragraph 2	The lake is the largest in the world ❷_____. • It is more than 1,600 meters deep and contains 20% of the world's ❸_____. • It is home to more than 1,000 unique species of plants and animals.
Paragraph 3	Lake Baikal is less well known than other natural wonders. • The ❹_____ is underpopulated, but the government is working to protect the lake.

by volume	natural wonders	surrounding region	fresh water

Reading Comprehension

Main Idea

1. **What is the passage mainly about?**

   a. common threats to the environment in Russia

   b. the reasons that Siberia is an underpopulated region

   c. ways the Russian government is reducing water pollution

   d. the characteristics of and work to protect the world's deepest lake

Details

2. **What does It in the first paragraph refer to?**

   a. Russia   b. the region of Siberia   c. the largest country   d. Lake Baikal

3. **Why is Lake Baikal the largest lake in the world by volume?**

   _____

4. **Which of the following is NOT true about Lake Baikal?**

   a. It is 72 kilometers in length.

   b. More than 300 streams and rivers flow into it.

   c. It is over 1,600 meters at its maximum point of depth.

   d. It is home to plants and animals that live nowhere else.

5. **Which of the following is true about the region around Lake Baikal?**

   a. It was discovered before 1643.

   b. Its population is about 25 million.

   c. Criminals were once exiled there.

   d. A paper mill has been pumping harmful waste into Baikal.

6. **What steps has the Russian government taken to protect Lake Baikal?**

   It has closed _____.

Inference

7. **What CANNOT be inferred from the passage?**

   a. There is a lot of undeveloped land in Siberia.

   b. There was an oil spill into the lake in the past.

   c. There are animal species that need protection in the region.

   d. There is more awareness of Lake Baikal's environmental value today.

12 Chapter 1

Summary

Use the phrases in the box to complete the summary.

| pollution and oil spills | unfrozen fresh water |
| deepest lake | vast region | species of plants |

Lake Baikal is situated in the ❶_____ of Siberia in Russia. This natural wonder of the world is also known as "The Blue Eye of Siberia." It is the ❷_____ in the world and the largest lake by volume, containing 20 percent of the world's ❸_____. Lake Baikal is home to many ❹_____ and animals, and hundreds of rivers and streams flow into it. Lake Baikal is very old but was not discovered until relatively recently. Because of threats from ❺_____, the Russian government has allocated more money to the lake's protection.

Language Focus

> **past participial phrase: (being +) p.p.**
> Participial phrases with past participles have a passive meaning. In a past participial phrase, *being* can be omitted.
> EX *(Being)* **Situated in Russia**, the region of Siberia is vast.

Rewrite the sentences by using participial phrase like the example in the box.

1. Because it was built of wood, the house was clearly a fire risk.
   ▶ _____

2. If it is looked after carefully, the plant can live through the winter.
   ▶ _____

3. Because she was annoyed by the boys' behavior, she complained to the principal.
   ▶ _____

The Harbor of Rio De Janeiro

▶ *As you read, consider how humans have altered the harbor of Rio de Janeiro.*

The natural wonders of the world change at a geological pace. It is difficult for humans to observe these changes. The Grand Canyon in the United States and Uluru in Australia would have looked a little different hundreds of thousands of years ago. Humans admire but rarely alter such landmarks. The harbor of Rio de Janeiro, however, is a modified natural wonder. But has it been enhanced or **debased** by human **intervention** in nature?

Natives had originally called the harbor Guanabara, which means "the arm of the sea." On New Year's Day 1502, Portuguese explorers discovered this huge natural harbor. In **recognition** of the month of their finding it, they called the harbor Rio de Janeiro, meaning the river of January. As the Portuguese sailed inland, a set of unusually-shaped rocks came into view. They named the highest one they saw *Corcovado* after what they thought it resembled — a **hunchback**.

In 1555, the French established a **colony** on one of the islands in the harbor. Just a year later, they were kicked out by Portuguese settlers. **They** established the city of Rio de Janeiro. It remained the capital of Brazil until 1960 when the capital was changed to Brasilia. Today, Rio de Janeiro is world famous for its beautiful beaches and mountain cable cars. The "hunchback" now carries a passenger: the statue of Christ the Redeemer. This 38-meter tall statue overlooks the harbor and is a symbol of Rio.

Nevertheless, Rio's harbor faces many threats. **Urbanization**, deforestation, and pollution are all damaging the landscape. Major oil spills have killed the mangrove trees there. Some estimate that 70 percent of Rio's sewage is dumped directly into Guanabara Bay. The government is taking steps to clean up the environment. One such step is the closure of one of the world's largest landfills, located near the harbor. However, many worry that human intervention has already done too much damage to this natural wonder. **Words 320**

▲ Statue of Christ the Redeemer

Vocabulary in Context

A **Match the words in bold from the passage with their correct definitions.**

1. _____ special attention given to an event
2. _____ a person with an unusually curved spine
3. _____ the act of becoming involved in an event
4. _____ to make something worse or lower in quality
5. _____ the process of an area becoming more developed like a city
6. _____ an area controlled by a country that is usually far away from it

B **Look at the underlined words in the passage and answer the questions.**

1. The word "pace" in the first paragraph is closest in meaning to _____.
   a. area   b. group   c. rate   d. step

2. The word "admire" in the first paragraph is closest in meaning to _____.
   a. value   b. modify   c. represent   d. describe

3. The word "face" in the fourth paragraph is closest in meaning to _____.
   a. measure   b. confront   c. lead   d. overlook

Reading Skill *The main idea of each paragraph gives a general idea that is explained in the rest of the paragraph.*

Fill in the chart with the phrases in the box.

Paragraph 1	The natural wonders of the world change at a geological pace, but the harbor of Rio de Janeiro has been modified by ❶_____.
Paragraph 2	Portuguese explorers discovered the harbor in 1502 and named it Rio de Janeiro, meaning the ❷_____.
Paragraph 3	The Portuguese ❸_____ of Rio de Janeiro in 1556 after expelling the French.
Paragraph 4	Threats ranging from urbanization to pollution are all damaging the harbor's ❹_____.

human intervention   natural environment   river of January   established the city

Unit 2 15

Reading Comprehension

Main Idea

1. **What is the passage mainly about?**

    a. how human action has altered and harmed Rio de Janeiro
    b. the various settlers and inhabitants of Rio throughout its history
    c. the government's plans to develop tourist attractions at Rio's harbor
    d. Rio's natural resources that have been destroyed because of pollution

Details

2. **What does Rio de Janeiro mean?**

   _____

3. **What does They in the third paragraph refer to?**

    a. islands   b. the French   c. native   d. Portuguese settlers

4. **According to the passage, which of the following is true?**

    a. Rio has been the capital of Brazil since 1960.
    b. Portuguese sailors called the harbor Rio de Janeiro.
    c. The French discovered *Corcovado* for the first time.
    d. The Portuguese settlers were the first to establish a colony in Rio.

5. **Why is the highest rock named *Corcovado*?**

   _____

6. **How is the government trying to protect Rio's harbor?**

    a. by closing a nearby landfill
    b. by planting more mangrove trees there
    c. by cleaning up the beaches for tourists
    d. by dumping less sewage in the harbor

Inference

7. **What can be inferred from the passage?**

    a. Rio de Janeiro has a lot of statues throughout the city.
    b. Some of the islands in the harbor remained a French colony.
    c. Portuguese explorers built a statue of Christ the Redeemer.
    d. People were not concerned with protecting the harbor in the past.

Summary

Use the phrases in the box to complete the summary.

	the capital of Brazil	has been modified
French colonizers	reduce the damage	geological pace

The natural wonders of the world usually change at a ❶_____, but the harbor of Rio de Janeiro ❷_____ by human design. In January 1502, Portuguese explorers discovered the harbor and named it Rio de Janeiro, meaning the river of January. After kicking out ❸_____, the Portuguese established the city of Rio de Janeiro in 1556. The city was ❹_____ until 1960. These days, Rio's harbor is famous for its beaches, mountain cable cars, and the statue of Christ the Redeemer. Even so, Rio's harbor is threatened by urbanization, deforestation, and oil spills. While the government is trying to ❺_____ to the environment, many fear that too much damage has already been done.

Language Focus

non-defining relative clause

Non-defining relative clauses are used to add extra information about the person or thing. We don't use *that* to introduce a non-defining relative clause.

EX *Natives had called the harbor Guanabara, <u>and it</u> means "the arm of the sea."*
   = *Natives had called the harbor Guanabara, **which** means "the arm of the sea."*

Rewrite the sentences by using relative pronouns like the example in the box.

1. They called the harbor Rio de Janeiro, and it means the river of January.
   ▶ _____

2. I recently talked to Mr. Richmond, and he lectures in art at the local college.
   ▶ _____

3. One step is the closure of one of the world's largest landfills, and it is located near the harbor.
   ▶ _____

Chapter 2
Social Issues

Unit 3   **The Global Refugee Crisis**

           Reading Skill | *Main Idea*
           Language Focus | *offer/lend/show + indirect object + direct object*

Unit 4   **Too Many College Graduates**

           Reading Skill | *Cause & Effect*
           Language Focus | *that/those*

Unit 3

One of the greatest problems facing the world today is the issue of refugees. These are people who have been forced to leave their homes. What are some reasons that people become refugees? How can organizations help refugees?

Unit 4

Many young people today are told that the best way to succeed in life is getting a college education. However, there can be problems if too many people graduate from college. What problems do you think having too many graduates can cause?

The Global Refugee Crisis

▶ As you read, try to understand why people become refugees and how the UN works to help these people.

For most of us, our lives are stable and generally happy. We can live in our homes safely and have regular access to food and water. But millions of people around the world do not have this option. Due to natural disasters or conflicts, these people have been **uprooted** from their homelands. These people are refugees, and it is the work of **humanitarian** organizations to support them.

Although the definition of a refugee is debated, the United Nations (UN) defines a refugee as someone who escapes to another region or country due to events that disturb public order. This includes **persecution** for reasons of race, religion, or nationality. People also flee due to pressure from outside forces and occupation by foreign militaries. The crises in Darfur, Sudan and Syria are examples of this.

The UN estimates that over 43 million people today are displaced. Around 15 million of these people are refugees. Another one million of them are **asylum seekers**. Asylum seekers differ from other types of refugees because they do not hold official refugee status yet. Among all refugees, the UN estimates that between 6 and 12 million are stateless. These people are not official citizens of any nation. As a result, they have nowhere to turn for help.

Fortunately, the UN currently assists millions of refugees globally. They do this by providing access to clean food and water. In some cases, they offer **sanitation** and healthcare services. In addition to giving short-term **relief**, the United Nations Relief and Works Agency (UNRWA) offers longer-term services to refugees. One such group is the 4.5 million Palestinian refugees throughout the Middle East. The UNRWA offers these people education and social services in addition to more general relief and health services.

With the help of the United Nations, millions of refugees can get the assistance they need to survive until they are able to establish more permanent homes.

Words 316

Vocabulary in Context

A **Match the words or phrases in bold from the passage with their correct definitions.**

1. _____ aid or assistance given to people in difficult situations
2. _____ to leave a place where you have lived for a long time
3. _____ relating to work that helps people improve their lives
4. _____ the act of treating people cruelly because of their beliefs
5. _____ a person seeking refugee status who hasn't got it yet
6. _____ the process of providing cleaning services such as collecting garbage

B **Look at the underlined words in the passage and answer the questions.**

1. The word "option" in the first paragraph is closest in meaning to _____.
   a. request   b. choice   c. lifestyle   d. reputation

2. The word "conflict" in the first paragraph is closest in meaning to _____.
   a. difference   b. repetition   c. battle   d. harmony

3. The word "assist" in the fourth paragraph is closest in meaning to _____.
   a. join   b. deny   c. support   d. generate

Reading Skill *The main idea of each paragraph gives a general idea that is explained in the rest of the paragraph.*

Fill in the chart with the phrases in the box.

Paragraph 1	Millions of people around the world are uprooted from ❶_____ due to natural disasters or conflicts.
Paragraph 2	A refugee is a person who flees his home due to ❷_____ from outside forces.
Paragraph 3	Over 43 million people around the world today ❸_____, with 15 million of them refugees and another one million of them asylum seekers.
Paragraph 4	The UN assists millions of refugees globally by ❹_____ to clean food and water along with offering sanitation and healthcare services.

persecution or pressure   are displaced   their homelands   providing access

Unit 3 21

Reading Comprehension

Main Idea

1. **What is the passage mainly about?**

   a. the effects of the crises in Darfur, Sudan and Syria
   b. which areas around the world have the most refugees
   c. how the UN works to stop persecution in the Middle East
   d. the definition of refugees and the types of aid they are given

Details

2. **What is the UN's definition of a refugee?**

   _____

3. **What does them in the third paragraph refer to?**

   a. refugees   b. citizens   c. displaced people   d. 15 million people

4. **Which of the following is true according to the passage?**

   a. Over 40 million people today are refugees.
   b. Asylum seekers have official refugee status.
   c. Stateless refugees can turn to any nation for help.
   d. People leave their countries to escape religious persecution.

5. **How does the UN help refugees?**

   It provides them with _____.

6. **How is the UNRWA different from other relief agencies?**

   a. It only operates in nations in the Middle East.
   b. It provides homes for refugees seeking asylum.
   c. It works mainly to help people displaced by wars.
   d. It provides additional services such as education to refugees.

Inference

7. **What CANNOT be inferred from the passage?**

   a. Most stateless refugees eventually receive assistance from the UN.
   b. The UN does not generally provide refugees with permanent homes.
   c. Refugees often come from nations with weak governments or militaries.
   d. People are sometimes mistreated because of their race, religion, or nationality.

Summary

Use the phrases in the box to complete the summary.

	uprooted from	leave their homeland
social services	humanitarian organizations	asylum seekers

Millions of people around the world are ❶ _____ their homelands due to disasters or conflicts. These people are refugees, and ❷ _____ such as the UN work to support them. The UN defines a refugee as someone who has been forced to ❸ _____ due to persecution or pressure from outside forces. Currently, over 43 million people are displaced globally. About 15 million of these people are refugees, while another million are ❹ _____. According to estimates, around 6 to 12 million refugees are stateless. The good news is that the UN assists millions of refugees around the world. They provide them with food, water, sanitation and healthcare services. In some areas, the UN provides education and ❺ _____ as well.

Language Focus

> **offer/lend/show + indirect object + direct object**
> → **offer/lend/show + direct object + to + indirect object**
>
> Some verbs are followed by two objects — one indirect object and one direct object.
> We can change the order of the objects if we put "to" before the indirect object.
>
> EX The UNRWA **offers** <u>refugees</u> <u>longer-term services</u>.
>   → The UNRWA **offers** <u>longer-term services</u> **to** <u>refugees</u>.

Rewrite the sentences like the example in the box.

1. You have to show the woman at the gate your ticket.
   ➤ _____

2. The UNRWA offers these people education and social services.
   ➤ _____

3. A lot of banks are unwilling to lend new businesses large amounts of money.
   ➤ _____

Too Many College Graduates

Unit 4

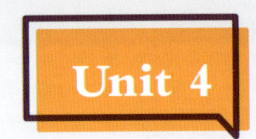

▶ *As you read, try to understand why having too many college graduates can be harmful for a nation.*

The United States, South Korea, and other countries face a shortage of workers in skilled jobs such as **welders**, electricians, and plumbers. At the same time, the unemployment rate among young adults **hovers** at 15 percent or more. How can this be? The reason is that too many young people in these countries are attending college even when they do not need a college degree.

Many stable, good-paying jobs require college degrees. Yet, when too many young people graduate from college, problems can arise. Studies estimate that only 25 percent of jobs today require college degrees. However, in the United States, more than 35 percent of people under the age of 30 are college graduates. This results in millions of young people working in low-salary jobs that often do not require college degrees or even high school diplomas. **Compounding** this issue is the fact that many students graduate from college with large amounts of debt. College graduates in America leave school with an average debt of $30,000. Students struggle to pay back their loans while working in jobs barely paying above the **minimum wage**.

While millions of people with college degrees have a hard time finding suitable jobs, thousands of skilled **labor** jobs go unfilled. Over 600,000 manufacturing jobs in the U.S. remain vacant due to a lack of skilled workers. Although these jobs pay well — the average hourly pay is $24 — few degree holders are willing to work them. One country has found a solution. Germany has a system that directs high school students who do not have the interest or ability to get a college degree toward **vocational** jobs. In fact, around half of German students get vocational training. The system is successful, as Germany's youth unemployment rate is only half that of similarly wealthy nations.

Getting an education is almost always beneficial. But not everybody needs to get a college degree to succeed in life.

Words 318

Vocabulary in Context

A **Match the words or phrases in bold from the passage with their correct definitions.**

1. _____ a person who works joining metal
2. _____ to stay near or hang around something
3. _____ relating to working, usually with the hands
4. _____ to add to something bad or to make it worse
5. _____ relating to skills, training, etc. needed for a particular job
6. _____ the lowest amount of money companies must pay their workers

B **Look at the underlined words in the passage and answer the questions.**

1. The word "shortage" in the first paragraph is closest in meaning to _____.
   a. lack   b. surplus   c. relief   d. concern

2. The word "arise" in the second paragraph is closest in meaning to _____.
   a. increase   b. calculate   c. work   d. occur

3. The word "vacant" in the third paragraph is closest in meaning to _____.
   a. employed   b. unoccupied   c. respected   d. proper

Reading Skill *Cause and effect is when one event causes something to happen. The cause explains why something happens, and the effect is what happens as a result.*

Fill in the chart with the phrases in the box.

Cause	Effect
More than 35 percent of young adults in the U.S. have a ❶_____.	Many of these young people cannot ❷_____ requiring college degrees.
Few degree holders are willing to work manufacturing jobs.	Over 600,000 skilled labor jobs ❸_____.
About half of German students are put into vocational training programs.	The country's youth ❹_____ is only half that of other countries.

| remain vacant | college degree | find jobs | unemployment rate |

Reading Comprehension

Main Idea

1 **What is the main idea of the passage?**

   a. It is becoming too easy for students to receive college degrees.

   b. Companies should create more jobs that require a college degree.

   c. Having too many people attend college can create problems for a nation.

   d. Germany has the best system for preparing young people for the job market.

Details

2 **Why are millions of young people working in low-salary jobs?**

   Because the number of college graduates _____

3 **Which of the following is true according to the passage?**

   a. The majority of young people today in America have college degrees.

   b. The unemployment rate among young adults is greater than 25 percent.

   c. There is currently greater demand for college graduates than skilled workers.

   d. Many college graduates in the U.S. cannot afford to repay their student loans.

4 **What does them in the third paragraph refer to?**

   a. suitable jobs   b. manufacturing jobs

   c. college degrees   d. skilled workers

5 **Why do many manufacturing jobs in the U.S. remain empty?**

   _____

6 **How is Germany's education system different from other countries' systems?**

   a. It forces young people to work in manufacturing jobs.

   b. It requires all students to learn how to do skilled labor jobs.

   c. It provides the same educational programs for all students.

   d. It encourages students who are not academic to receive vocational training.

Inference

7 **What can be inferred from the passage?**

   a. Many young people in the U.S. have vocational training.

   b. Germany has more skilled labor job vacancies than the United States.

   c. The number of plumbers and electricians will increase in the near future.

   d. College graduates think skilled labor jobs are inferior to jobs needing degrees.

Summary

Use the phrases in the box to complete the summary.

college degrees	vocational training	
skilled labor jobs	low-paying jobs	their student loans

Many nations are facing the problem of having too many college graduates. While only around 25 percent of jobs require ❶_____, more than 35 percent of young people have graduated from college in the U.S. As a result, millions of these young people end up working in ❷_____, making it difficult for these graduates to repay ❸_____. While college graduates struggle to find jobs requiring degrees, thousands of ❹_____ remain vacant. Germany seems to have a solution. It has a system that directs high school students who would not benefit from college into ❺_____. Consequently, Germany has one of the lowest youth unemployment rates of any wealthy nation.

Language Focus

that/those

We use *that/those* to avoid repeating a noun which has been mentioned before.

EX Germany's youth unemployment rate is only half **that** of similarly wealthy nations.
  = youth unemployment rate

Children understand familiar voices better than **those** of strangers.
  = voices

Rewrite the sentences by using *that* or *those* instead of the underlined words.

1. In my opinion, the finest wines are <u>wines</u> from Italy.
   ➤ _____

2. A dog's intelligence is much greater than <u>the intelligence</u> of a cat.
   ➤ _____

3. Hemingway's novels are more entertaining than <u>novels</u> of Dickens.
   ➤ _____

Chapter 3
Art & People

Unit 5 **Andy Warhol, Inventor of Pop Art**

Reading Skill | *Sequencing*
Language Focus | *perfect participial phrase: having + p.p.*

Unit 6 **What Is Pop Music?**

Reading Skill | *Main Idea*
Language Focus | *substitute word "one"*

Unit 5

Artist Andy Warhol is widely considered to be the inventor of pop art. He began making artwork after working in the advertising industry. What do you think pop art is? How do you think Warhol's experience in advertising affected his works?

Unit 6

The most popular genre of music today is pop music. Artists ranging from The Beatles to Taylor Swift are all considered pop musicians. Where do you think pop music originally comes from? Why do you think it is so popular today?

Andy Warhol, Inventor of Pop Art

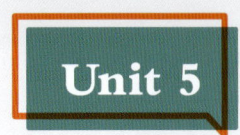

Unit 5

▶ As you read, think about how Warhol's art is similar to consumer products.

Andy Warhol was born in 1928 in the industrial town of Pittsburgh, where his father, an immigrant from Slovakia, worked as a coal miner. Warhol attended a Catholic school but was frequently sick. He suffered from **disorders** and spent many days in bed listening to the radio and collecting pictures of movie stars. After high school, he attended the Carnegie Institute of Technology and then moved to New York in 1949. In the 1950s, he worked as a **commercial** artist in magazine illustrating and advertising. He used his creativity to sell other people's things. In the 1960s, he used his creativity to sell his own things.

Warhol took commonly used consumer items, such as Coca-Cola bottles and cans of soup, and created **mass-produced** images of them. He was reselling images of things that were for sale in supermarkets everywhere, presenting these products as they are. For instance, he called his prints of soup cans *Campbell's Soup Cans* and his prints of cola bottles *Green Coca-Cola Bottles*. His art studio was called the Factory, which was where he constantly **churned out** his works in the same way that factories produce their products. It was there that he made pop art.

Warhol made images of twentieth-century American life that became part of pop culture. His most iconic image of a famous personality was a *screen print of Marilyn Monroe, a popular American actress in the 1950s and 1960s. His image of Monroe is still found on T-shirts, bags, and other products today. Warhol was also famous for not wishing to explain his art in depth. He once said that it was all "surface" and that "There's nothing behind it."

Warhol remained a **prolific** artist until his death in 1987, having produced over 1,500 works throughout his life. Today, the Andy Warhol Museum in Pittsburgh is the largest museum in the United States **devoted** to a single artist. **Words 316**

▲ Marilyn Monroe

*screen print: an image produced by printing designs onto clothing using ink and screens

Vocabulary in Context

A Match the words or phrases in bold from the passage with their correct definitions.

1. _____ concerned with making a profit
2. _____ made in large numbers, usually in a factory
3. _____ to create a product quickly in large numbers
4. _____ to use something for a single or special purpose
5. _____ a condition of the body or the mind that is not healthy
6. _____ describing someone who has produced many novels, artworks, etc.

B Look at the underlined words in the passage and answer the questions.

1. The word "illustrate" in the first paragraph is closest in meaning to _____.
   a. indicate   b. edit   c. draw   d. publish

2. The word "commonly" in the second paragraph is closest in meaning to _____.
   a. typically   b. surprisingly   c. lately   d. rarely

3. The word "present" in the second paragraph is closest in meaning to _____.
   a. conserve   b. display   c. organize   d. develop

Reading Skill *Sequencing is putting events in order from first to last. When we sequence, we can easily understand which events happen first, second, and so on.*

Fill in the chart and number the events in order.

	Warhol was a ❶_____ until his death in 1987.
	The images he made of twentieth-century American life became part of ❷_____.
	He worked in the ❸_____ as an illustrator and advertiser.
	Andy Warhol spent his youth collecting ❹_____.
	He created ❺_____ of commonly used consumer items, such as Coca-Cola bottles and Campbell's soup cans.

	pictures of celebrities	prolific artist
pop culture	mass-produced images	magazine industry

Reading Comprehension

Main Idea

1. **What is the passage mainly about?**
   a. the hard time Warhol had dealing with illness during his childhood
   b. some of the most famous pieces of artwork created by Andy Warhol
   c. the reasons that Andy Warhol liked using iconic images in his artworks
   d. Andy Warhol's life experiences and the works he became famous for producing

Details

2. **Why did Warhol call his art studio the Factory?**
   a. Because it was in an old factory
   b. Because he mass-produced art there
   c. Because he wanted to work in a factory
   d. Because it was in an area of the city with many factories

3. **What does it in the third paragraph refer to?**
   a. his art   b. iconic image   c. pop culture   d. his image of Monroe

4. **What does "There's nothing behind it" in the third paragraph mean?**
   Warhol meant that _____.

5. **According to the passage, which of the following is true?**
   a. Warhol painted a picture of Marilyn Monroe.
   b. Warhol's art museum is located in New York City.
   c. Warhol sold his artwork to advertising companies.
   d. Warhol's artwork is still found on products today.

6. **What is significant about the Andy Warhol Museum?**
   _____

Inference

7. **What CANNOT be inferred from the passage?**
   a. Warhol was interested in pop culture from a young age.
   b. Many of Warhol's pieces sold for large amounts of money.
   c. Warhol made artworks using images that were already popular.
   d. Warhol was frequently absent from school because of his illness.

Summary

Use the phrases in the box to complete the summary.

| mass-produced items | a single artist |
| commercial artist | no deeper meaning | media and celebrities |

From a young age, Andy Warhol was interested in ❶_____. After attending the Carnegie Institute of Technology, Warhol moved to New York to work as a ❷_____. In the 1960s, he began selling his own works. He made works of art out of ❸_____ such as Coca-Cola bottles and Campbell's soup cans. He called these works pop art. Many of Warhol's pieces became part of American pop culture. One of the most recognized is a screen print he made of Marilyn Monroe. When describing his work, Warhol said that it was all "surface" with ❹_____. Today, the Andy Warhol Museum in his hometown of Pittsburgh is the largest U.S. museum dedicated to ❺_____.

Language Focus

perfect participial phrase: having + p.p.

When one action happens before another action, we use *having + p.p.* for the first action.

EX *Warhol remained a prolific artist until his death in 1987, **having produced** over 1,500 works throughout his life.*

Rewrite the sentences by using participial phrase like the example in the box.

1. Because she had spent her childhood in Berlin, she knew the city well.
    ▶ _____

2. After we had found a hotel, we looked for some place to have dinner.
    ▶ _____

3. Because I had already seen the movie twice, I didn't want to go again with my friends.
    ▶ _____

What Is Pop Music?

Unit 6

▶ Pay attention to how pop music developed and what its characteristics are as you read.

The Beatles, Michael Jackson, and Britney Spears: What do these musicians have in common? They all have had a major influence on the development of modern popular music, otherwise known as pop music. Pop music refers to a wide range of musicians and styles. However, all pop music has a clear origin and distinctive characteristics.

The term pop music originated in the 1920s in the United States. At that time, the term referred simply to any song with popular appeal. Early pop songs were influenced by many genres ranging from ballads, jazz and country. Today, pop music is generally defined as any music that is distinct from classical, jazz, and rock music.

Since the 1960s, pop music has been **aimed at** teenagers and young adults. Most pop songs are professionally produced and medium in tempo and in length, usually around two-and-a-half to four minutes long. The main instruments are human voices and **synthesizers**. Pop songs have good rhythms and simple structures. Most songs feature a catchy **hook** followed by **verses** and a chorus with lyrics that deal with love and relationships. Using such a structure, pop music aims to appeal to as many people as possible.

Despite the broad appeal of pop music, many regional varieties have developed. One of the most notable examples of this is Europop. This genre of music usually has a faster tempo than general pop music and is more dance-**oriented** as a result. Two other sub-genres of pop are Japanese pop and Korean pop, otherwise known as J-Pop and K-Pop. These genres were originally influenced by Western pop groups such as The Beatles and the Beach Boys.

Today, pop music remains one of the most widely played types of music. Some criticize pop music for being a **corporate** genre of music, not one resulting from artistic feelings or creativity. Nevertheless, pop music will likely top the charts for years to come.

Words 316

Vocabulary in Context

A Match the words or phrases in bold from the passage with their correct definitions.

1. _____ concerned with or focused on
2. _____ related to companies rather than individuals
3. _____ a specific section or part of a song, poem, etc.
4. _____ to focus on a specific person, group, thing, etc.
5. _____ a machine that uses computers to imitate instruments
6. _____ the part of a song, story, etc. that gets a person's attention

B Look at the underlined words in the passage and answer the questions.

1. The word "distinct" in the second paragraph is closest in meaning to _____.
   a. different   b. disturbing   c. indefinite   d. noticeable

2. The word "catchy" in the third paragraph is closest in meaning to _____.
   a. interesting   b. dull   c. memorable   d. ignorant

3. The word "regional" in the fourth paragraph is closest in meaning to _____.
   a. local   b. native   c. particular   d. overall

Reading Skill *The main idea of each paragraph gives a general idea that is explained in the rest of the paragraph.*

Fill in the chart with the phrases in the box.

Paragraph 1	Pop music refers to a wide variety of musicians and styles, but it has ❶_____ and characteristics.
Paragraph 2	Pop music originated ❷_____ in the 1920s and was influenced by ballads, jazz, and country.
Paragraph 3	Most pop songs share the same characteristics, being ❸_____ that have good rhythms and simple structures.
Paragraph 4	❹_____ of pop music have developed, including Europop, J-Pop, and K-Pop.

| in the U.S. | regional varieties | a clear origin | medium tempo songs |

Unit 6 35

Reading Comprehension

Main Idea

1. **What is the main idea of the passage?**

   a. Pop music today has become too commercialized.
   b. Today's pop music is quite different from 1960's pop music.
   c. All pop music shares a common origin and characteristics.
   d. Different parts of the world have their own types of pop music.

Details

2. **What is the definition of pop music today?**

   _____

3. **According to the passage, which of the following is NOT true?**

   a. The term pop music was made in the 1960s.
   b. Most pop songs are less than four minutes long.
   c. Pop music generally targets teenagers and young adults.
   d. The main instruments in pop songs are voices and synthesizers.

4. **Why do pop songs have good rhythms and simple structures with a catchy hook?**

   _____

5. **What does this in the fourth paragraph refer to?**

   a. pop music   b. broad appeal   c. music genre   d. regional variety

6. **Which of the following is true about Europop according to the passage?**

   a. It is similar to general pop music.
   b. It is intended to be dance music.
   c. It has a slower tempo than other pop music.
   d. It originated from Western pop groups such as The Beatles.

Inference

7. **What can be inferred from the passage?**

   a. J-Pop and K-Pop are dance-oriented.
   b. Pop music is becoming less popular these days.
   c. Early pop songs were mainly produced for young adults.
   d. Pop music is often created by corporations and not singers.

36 Chapter 3

Summary

Use the phrases in the box to complete the summary.

	lacking creativity	good rhythms
faster tempo	early pop songs	aimed at teenagers

Pop music refers to a wide range of musicians and styles, yet all pop music shares the same origin and characteristics. ❶_____ were influenced by ballads, jazz, and country. Since the 1960s, most pop music has been ❷_____ and young adults. Pop songs are usually medium-length, medium-tempo songs that have ❸_____ and catchy hooks. This structure is meant to appeal to many people, but regional varieties have developed. One such example is Europop, which usually has a ❹_____ and is more dance-oriented than regular pop music. Two other popular sub-genres are Japanese and Korean pop. While some criticize pop music for ❺_____, it will likely remain at the top of the music charts for years to come.

Language Focus

> **substitute word *one***
>
> We can use *one* instead of repeating a singular countable noun. We use *ones* for a plural noun.
>
> EX *Some criticize pop music for being a corporate genre of music, not **one** resulting from artistic feelings.*
> = a genre of music

Replace the underlined words with *one* or *ones* and rewrite the sentences.

1. The hotel that we had booked turned out to be a luxury <u>hotel</u>.
   ▶ _____

2. Normally I don't like wearing a scarf, but it was so cold that I put <u>a scarf</u> on.
   ▶ _____

3. I answered most of the questions, but had to skip some very difficult <u>questions</u>.
   ▶ _____

Unit 6   37

Chapter 4
Food & Environment

Unit 7 Staple Foods Around the World

Reading Skill | *Main Idea & Details*
Language Focus | *perfect infinitive: to + have + p.p.*

Unit 8 Free-Range Farming

Reading Skill | *Cause & Effect*
Language Focus | *be allowed/asked/expected + to-infinitive*

Unit 7

What are some foods you eat every day? Most likely, you would say rice, wheat, corn or other similar types of food. What do these types of foods have in common? Why do you think they are so widely eaten?

Unit 8

These days, people want to eat healthier food. In response to this, some farmers are changing their farms to free-range farms. This is a type of farming where the animals are supposedly treated better than livestock raised on traditional farms. How do you think free-range farming differs from traditional farming?

Staple Foods Around the World

▶ *While you read, think about the characteristics that all staple foods have in common.*

What are some foods you eat every day? Depending on where you live in the world, your diet probably contains considerable amounts of rice, wheat, or corn. These foods are referred to as **staples** because they are a **dominant** portion of many people's diets.

Staple foods have many characteristics in common. They are generally plant based, inexpensive, and readily available. They also contain three or more **macronutrients** considered essential for health: carbohydrates, proteins, and fats. In early societies, staples needed to be long lasting as well as nutritious. The reason was they often needed to be stored for months without decaying. Although this is no longer a concern in most countries, our staple foods have not changed much. Over 50,000 **edible** plant species are known to exist, but just 15 types of plants comprise 90 percent of the world's food supply not including meat.

The most produced crop in the world is maize, otherwise known as corn. First grown in Central America over 10,000 years ago, maize is the most widely grown crop in the United States today. China, Brazil, and Mexico also produce large amounts of it. Rice is the main staple in Asia but is widely eaten throughout the world. In fact, it is the main staple food for over half the world's population. Scientists believe it was first **cultivated** in either Australia or China and was introduced to the West via trade. Rice grows best in warm, wet regions, such as those around the Ganges River and the Mekong River. The third main staple food is wheat, thought to have come from the Fertile Crescent located south of Turkey from Egypt to Iraq. Wheat thrives in areas with **temperate** climates and is mainly grown in China, India, the United States, and Russia.

While people in wealthier countries are eating increasing amounts of meat, staple foods such as maize and rice continue to comprise a major part of our diets. **Words 322**

Vocabulary in Context

A Match the words in bold from the passage with their correct definitions.

1. _____ safe for eating
2. _____ to grow or raise crops for food
3. _____ taking up the largest part; primary
4. _____ an important nutrient necessary for good health
5. _____ used to describe a climate that is not too hot or too cold
6. _____ an important food that makes up a large portion of our diets

B Look at the underlined words in the passage and answer the questions.

1. The word "readily" in the second paragraph is closest in meaning to _____.
   a. carefully   b. occasionally   c. easily   d. conventionally

2. The word "store" in the second paragraph is closest in meaning to _____.
   a. purchase   b. gather   c. bring   d. keep

3. The word "fertile" in the third paragraph is closest in meaning to _____.
   a. furious   b. productive   c. famous   d. persuasive

Reading Skill   *The main idea is usually at the beginning of a text and makes a general statement. The supporting details are specific ideas that support the main idea.*

Fill in the chart with the phrases in the box.

Paragraph 2	Staple foods have many characteristics in common. • They contain three or more essential macronutrients. • They need to be stored for several months ❶_____.
Paragraph 3	There are three main types of staple foods. • Maize is the most ❷_____ in the world. It was first grown 10,000 years ago in Central America, and is commonly grown in America, China, and Mexico today. • Rice is widely eaten but is most popular in Asia. It was first grown in either Australia or China, and grows well in ❸_____. • Wheat is the third main staple grown in the Fertile Crescent. It grows best in areas with ❹_____.

warm, wet regions   produced crop   temperate climates   without decaying

Unit 7 41

Reading Comprehension

Main Idea

1. **What is the passage mainly about?**

   a. how to grow different types of crops that will last long

   b. the ways that staple foods have spread across the world

   c. reasons people's primary staple foods have changed in recent years

   d. the small number of plant-based foods that make up most of people's diets

Details

2. **Why are rice, wheat, and corn called staple foods?**

   _____

3. **What does this in the second paragraph refer to?**

   a. being nutritious   b. decaying   c. being long lasting   d. macronutrient

4. **Which of the following is NOT true according to the passage?**

   a. Staple foods have three or more macronutrients.

   b. The majority of plant species are widely eaten.

   c. It is possible to store staple foods for several months.

   d. Most staple foods are not expensive and widely available.

5. **Which of the following is true about the most popular staple foods in the passage?**

   a. Rice was first cultivated in Central America.

   b. Wheat grows best in warm areas with wet climates.

   c. A majority of people eat wheat as their main staple food.

   d. More maize is grown in the U.S. than any other type of crop.

6. **Where was wheat originally grown?**

   _____

Inference

7. **What can be inferred from the passage?**

   a. Meat is becoming a staple food in wealthier countries.

   b. India and Thailand are major wheat-producing countries.

   c. People's eating habits have not changed much over time.

   d. Rice used to be more widely grown than maize used to be.

Summary

Use the phrases in the box to complete the summary.

> food supply the Fertile Crescent
> dominant portion readily available more than half

An important part of everyone's diet around the world is staple foods. Foods such as rice and wheat make up a ❶_____ of many people's diets. Most staple foods are plant based, inexpensive, and ❷_____. They usually contain macronutrients such as carbohydrates, proteins, and fats. While over 50,000 types of edible plants exist, only 15 types comprise most of the world's ❸_____. The most common food is maize and it is the most widely grown crop in the United States. Rice is the main staple food for ❹_____ the people in the world. It grows best in the regions around the Ganges River and the Mekong River with wet and warm climates. Wheat is the third major staple food. It originated from ❺_____, and today is primarily grown in regions with temperate climates.

Language Focus

> **perfect infinitive: to + have + p.p.**
> Perfect infinitives can be used to show action earlier than the verb.
>
> EX Over 50,000 edible plant species are known **to exist**.
>   → It *is* known that over 50,000 edible plant species *exist*.
>   Wheat is thought **to have come** from the Fertile Crescent.
>   → It *is* thought that wheat *came* from the Fertile Crescent.

Choose the correct one so that two sentences have the same meaning.

1. It seems that they forgot about the meeting.

   = They seem (to forget / to have forgotten) about the meeting.

2. He pretended that he had lost her phone number.

   = He pretended (to lose / to have lost) her phone number.

3. It is reported that the stolen painting is worth $20 million.

   = The stolen painting is reported (to be / to have been) worth $20 million.

Free-Range Farming

▶ *While you read, pay attention to the pros and cons of free-range farming.*

All over the world today, people are becoming more conscious of eating healthy. This has led to the rise in organic farming, referring to crop production without pesticides. A related concept is free-range farming. People believe that free-range farming is more **humane** to the animals and the animals are healthier to eat, but is this really the case?

Free-range farming has a different meaning in most countries. But in general it refers to a farming system where the animals are allowed to spend at least some time outdoors during the daytime to **roam**. This is beneficial for the animals in many ways. It allows them to get exercise, making them stronger, and lets them **forage** for food. Also, sunlight provides them with vitamin D, an important nutrient for all living creatures. In contrast, conventionally raised livestock spend their entire lives trapped in tiny cages barely larger than their bodies. They live in a climate controlled environment and never see the sun. Free-range livestock are often organically raised. This means that they are not given the growth hormones or antibiotics that livestock on factory farms often get. The result is, in theory, meat and dairy products that are both healthier and tastier.

However, critics point out that the term free range, especially in the United States, is vague. There is no requirement **specifying** how often or how long the animals must stay outdoors to be labeled as free range. Also, because free-range animals do not receive antibiotics, they are more **susceptible** to diseases. Often when a free-range animal becomes sick or infected, it is killed rather than being given medication. Furthermore, many free-range animals are killed in the same **slaughterhouses** that factory-farmed livestock is killed in. This calls into question whether free-range farming is really more humane.

Free-range farming is a good idea in theory. But it needs to be regulated to ensure that these farm animals receive the proper treatment they deserve. **Words 322**

Vocabulary in Context

A Match the words in bold from the passage with their correct definitions.

1. _____ morally correct; ethical
2. _____ to search an area for food
3. _____ a place where animals are killed for food
4. _____ to walk around an area with no particular purpose
5. _____ easily affected or injured by something; vulnerable
6. _____ to outline or establish a set of rules for doing something

B Look at the underlined words in the passage and answer the questions.

1. The word "trap" in the second paragraph is closest in meaning to _____.
   a. lock in   b. shut out   c. set down   d. turn off

2. The word "vague" in the third paragraph is closest in meaning to _____.
   a. unknown   b. complicated   c. unclear   d. specific

3. The word "ensure" in the fourth paragraph is closest in meaning to _____.
   a. deny   b. promote   c. invade   d. guarantee

Reading Skill *Cause and effect is when one event causes something to happen. The cause explains why something happens, and the effect is what happens as a result.*

Fill in the chart with the phrases in the box.

Cause	Effect
Free-range animals are given time to ❶_____ each day.	The animals ❷_____ and are able to forage for food.
Animals on free-range farms are not given growth hormones or antibiotics.	The meat and dairy products from these animals are ❸_____.
Free-range farm animals ❹_____ or infected.	They are usually killed rather than given medicine.

| get exercise | healthier and tastier | roam outside | become sick |

Unit 8   45

Reading Comprehension

Main Idea

1. **What is the main idea of the passage?**

   a. People should eat only livestock raised on free-range farms.
   b. It is better to raise farm animals without the use of antibiotics.
   c. Livestock are generally happier when they spend their lives outdoors.
   d. Free-range farming sounds healthier but needs to be regulated more.

Details

2. **What does free-range farming refer to according to the passage?**

   _____

3. **What does It in the second paragraph refer to?**

   a. roaming outdoors   b. daytime   c. animal   d. farming system

4. **Which of the following is true according to the passage?**

   a. Free-range animals spend all their time outdoors.
   b. Animals cannot survive without being exposed to vitamin D.
   c. Conventionally raised livestock roam outside for food during the daytime.
   d. The temperature is controlled in the cages of animals on conventional farms.

5. **Why are meat and dairy products from free-range animals considered to be healthier?**

   _____

6. **What is one of the main criticisms of free-range farming?**

   a. Animals on free-range farms stay outside for too long.
   b. Free-range farm animals are not killed in slaughterhouses.
   c. Too many antibiotics are given to free-range farm animals.
   d. It is not humane to kill animals rather than give them medicine.

Inference

7. **What CANNOT be inferred from the passage?**

   a. Allowing animals to roam outdoors makes them healthier.
   b. The United States does not have strong regulations for free-range farming.
   c. Free-range farm animals usually live longer than conventionally raised animals.
   d. Free-range farming will probably become more popular because people are more aware of healthy eating.

Summary

Use the phrases in the box to complete the summary.

too vague	forage for food	
receive antibiotics	part of their days	from the sun

Due to the rise in healthy eating habits among people around the world, free-range farming has become more popular. This refers to a farming system where the animals are allowed to spend at least ❶_____ outside roaming. This is beneficial since the animals get exercise and are able to ❷_____. They also get much needed vitamin D ❸_____. Free-range animals are also often raised without growth hormones or antibiotics, meaning that their meat is healthier and tastier. Yet, critics argue that the term free range is ❹_____. It does not specify how long animals must stay outside to be considered free range. Also, because free-range livestock do not ❺_____, they are likely to get sick or infected.

Language Focus

---
active: allow/ask/expect + object + to-infinitive

passive: be allowed/asked/expected + to-infinitive

EX It *allows* them *to get* exercise.
→ They **are allowed to get** exercise.

Rewrite the sentences by using the passive like the example in the box.

1. I asked John to mail those letters tomorrow.
   ➤ _____

2. We expect the renovation to be completed by the end of August.
   ➤ _____

3. They allow the animals to spend some time outdoors during the daytime.
   ➤ _____

Chapter 5
Science

Unit 9 | The Spaceship Cemetery

Reading Skill | *Main Idea*
Language Focus | *much/far/even/a lot + comparatives*

Unit 10 | Ancient Chinese and Egyptian Astronomy

Reading Skill | *Compare & Contrast*
Language Focus | *prepositions + which*

Unit 9

When spaceships are no longer able to be used, they need to be decommissioned. When this happens, scientists crash the ships into a place called the Spaceship Cemetery. Why do you think scientists crash the ships into this specific spot?

Unit 10

Astronomers today use highly advanced equipment to study outer space. Scientists in ancient societies did not have such advanced equipment available to them, yet were still able to know much about the sky. How do you think ancient people studied space? How do you think they could have used the information they learned?

The Spaceship Cemetery

Unit 9

▶ *As you read, consider the location of the Spaceship Cemetery and how scientists make the ships crash there.*

In the Southern Pacific Ocean lies one of the largest **cemeteries** in the world. But you will not find the graves of humans or animals there. All you will find are **decommissioned** spaceships. This is the Spaceship Cemetery.

The Spaceship Cemetery is located at the Oceanic Pole of **Inaccessibility**. This is the point on Earth located farthest away from any landmass. It is 3,200 kilometers north of Antarctica and almost 5,000 kilometers east of New Zealand. This spot was chosen for the obvious reason that there is almost no chance of **debris** crashing into populated areas. Spaceships landing in the area have less than a one-in-10,000 chance of impact with humans.

When decommissioning a spacecraft, scientists use Earth's **gravitational** pull to bring it down. The craft are gradually dragged closer and closer to the surface because of Earth's gravity. By using physics, scientists can cause a spacecraft to crash in the Spaceship Cemetery with high accuracy. Russia was the first to crash a spacecraft there in 1971. Since that time, hundreds of rocket boosters, spy satellites, and other objects from many countries have been crashed at the site. The largest object crashed at the site is the 142-ton Russian space station MIR, which was decommissioned in 2001.

Crashing MIR into the Spaceship Cemetery was a substantial challenge for scientists. Yet, an even greater challenge lies ahead: the future decommissioning of the International Space Station (ISS). Almost four times larger than MIR, the ISS is over 100 meters long and weighs more than 500 tons. It will come crashing down into the Pacific Ocean after it is decommissioned in 2028. Scientists will need to make extensive calculations to ensure that all the debris lands in the water.

One old saying claims that, "What goes up must come down." Likewise, nearly all of the world's **meticulously** engineered spacecraft will eventually find their way to a watery grave in the Spaceship Cemetery.

Words 319

Vocabulary in Context

A Match the words in bold from the passage with their correct definitions.

1. _____ with great care or detail
2. _____ a place where the dead are buried
3. _____ the state of not being able to reach
4. _____ small pieces that have separated from a larger object
5. _____ describing a ship that is no longer being officially used
6. _____ relating to gravity, which is the force that causes things to fall toward Earth

B Look at the underlined words in the passage and answer the questions.

1. The word "impact" in the second paragraph is closest in meaning to _____.
   a. statement   b. effect   c. collision   d. accident

2. The word "drag" in the third paragraph is closest in meaning to _____.
   a. trap   b. pull   c. bother   d. float

3. The word "substantial" in the fourth paragraph is closest in meaning to _____.
   a. considerable   b. minimal   c. accepted   d. critical

Reading Skill *The main idea of each paragraph gives a general idea that is explained in the rest of the paragraph.*

Fill in the chart with the phrases in the box.

Paragraph 1	The Southern Pacific Ocean is home to the Spaceship Cemetery, where ❶_____ go to die.
Paragraph 2	The cemetery is located at the Oceanic Pole of Inaccessibility, chosen because there is almost no chance of debris crashing into ❷_____.
Paragraph 3	Scientists use Earth's ❸_____ to drag ships closer to the surface and have them crash with great accuracy.
Paragraph 4	The future decommissioning of the International Space Station will require ❹_____ to crash all the debris safely.

extensive calculations	populated areas
decommissioned spaceships	gravitational pull

Unit 9 51

Reading Comprehension

Main Idea

1. **What is the best title for the passage?**

    a. Why the Russians Were the First to Decommission Spacecraft

    b. A Remote Part of the Pacific Ocean Where Spaceships Go to Die

    c. Accidents That Have Occurred When Decommissioning Spaceships

    d. The Challenge of Decommissioning the International Space Station

Details

2. **Why is the Spaceship Cemetery located at the Oceanic Pole of Inaccessibility?**

    It is located there because _____.

3. **According to the passage, which of the following is NOT true?**

    a. The largest object crashed at the site is MIR.

    b. All of the spacecraft in the cemetery belong to Russia.

    c. Decommissioned spacecraft are pulled to Earth by gravity.

    d. The cemetery is closer to Antarctica than it is to New Zealand.

4. **What does It in the fourth paragraph refer to?**

    a. MIR   b. the ISS   c. challenge   d. the Spaceship Cemetery

5. **How large is the International Space Station?**

    _____

6. **How will scientists work to crash the ISS safely?**

    a. by crashing it into MIR

    b. by aiming it to crash into Antarctica

    c. by making a huge number of calculations

    d. by getting help from the Russian government

Inference

7. **What can be inferred from the passage?**

    a. Not all Spacecraft Eventually return to Earth.

    b. The Spaceship Cemetery has been used since 2001.

    c. Most of the objects in the cemetery are rocket boosters.

    d. Scientists have already calculated how to crash the ISS.

Summary

Use the phrases in the box to complete the summary.

> drag the craft   a greater challenge
> its inaccessibility   landing in the cemetery   Southern Pacific Ocean

In the middle of the ❶_____ lies one of the largest cemeteries in the world. It is the Spaceship Cemetery, where decommissioned spacecraft go to die. The location was chosen because of ❷_____. Debris ❸_____ has a less than one-in-10,000 chance of crashing into populated areas. To decommission a spacecraft, scientists rely on Earth's gravitational pull to ❹_____ toward the surface. Since 1971, hundreds of old rocket boosters, spy satellites, and small space stations have been crashed there. The largest object to be crashed there is the Russian space station MIR. However, ❺_____ lies ahead, when the International Space Station will be crashed in the cemetery after its decommissioning in 2028.

Language Focus

> **much/far/even/a lot + comparatives**
> We cannot use *very* with comparatives. Instead we use *much, far, even, a lot,* etc.
> EX Yet, an **even** <u>greater</u> challenge lies ahead: the future decommissioning of the ISS.

Rewrite the sentences to include the given words.

1. Her illness was more serious than we thought at first. (far)
   ▶ _____

2. The shops are always more crowded just before Christmas. (much)
   ▶ _____

3. It's easier to learn a foreign language in a country where it is spoken. (a lot)
   ▶ _____

Ancient Chinese and Egyptian Astronomy

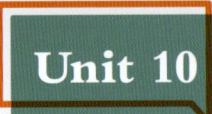

▶ *As you read, compare the methods and purposes of ancient Chinese and Egyptian astronomy.*

Astronomers today rarely look through telescopes. Rather, modern telescopes send an object's light to a computer, which then forms an image of the planet or star. Telescopes in space make images from X-rays and gamma rays gathered before they reach Earth's atmosphere. Astronomers also use other kinds of waves, such as radio and infrared light. All of **them** build pictures of the planets and stars in the universe. None of this technology was available to astronomers thousands of years ago. Even so, the cultures of ancient China and Egypt studied astronomy and were able to make sophisticated and complex observations about the objects they saw in the night sky.

Ancient Chinese astronomers were superstitious. They believed the appearance of a dragon **constellation** preceded the rainy season. However, they carefully noted what they saw in the sky. They worked to map and **catalog** every observable star. The *Chinese Classic of History* recorded a solar eclipse in 2137 BCE. Later, the Chinese constructed large **observatories**. From these, many astronomical phenomena were recorded. In 613 BCE, Halley's Comet was seen, and in 532 BCE, an exploding star, called a nova, was recorded. Other events such as sunspots and meteor showers also attracted the attention of Chinese astronomers.

▲ radio telescope

In Egyptian culture, astronomers were **revered**, playing a priestly role in Egyptian society. It was also their job to provide essential information to farmers since astronomy and agriculture were linked. Astronomers were expected, for example, to predict the approximate date on which the Nile River would flood. This was observed as occurring at the time of year when the sun appears to be farthest north. Egyptian astronomers devised a solar calendar of 365 days and divided it into 12 months of around 30 days each. The sky was divided into five constellations. Even the kings' **burial** places, the pyramids, were **aligned** with the position of the stars in the night sky.

▲ meteor shower

Words 315

Vocabulary in Context

A **Match the words in bold from the passage with their correct definitions.**

1. _____ to be in a line with something
2. _____ to respect and admire greatly
3. _____ to record information in a list
4. _____ a place where astronomers observe the sky
5. _____ the act of putting a dead body into a grave
6. _____ a group of stars that appears to form an image

B **Look at the underlined words in the passage and answer the questions.**

1. The word "sophisticated" in the first paragraph is closest in meaning to _____.
   a. hasty   b. conventional   c. advanced   d. insignificant

2. The word "approximate" in the third paragraph is closest in meaning to _____.
   a. unclear   b. precise   c. mysterious   d. estimated

3. The word "devise" in the third paragraph is closest in meaning to _____.
   a. create   b. suggest   c. predict   d. apply

Reading Skill *Comparing and contrasting is a way to explain how two or more things are similar and different.*

Fill in the chart with the phrases in the box.

Chinese Astronomers	Egyptian Astronomers
• Chinese astronomers attempted to ❶_____.	• Egyptian astronomers played ❹_____.
• They constructed ❷_____ to observe the heavens.	• They provided ❺_____ to farmers.
• They recorded ❸_____ like Halley's Comet and a nova.	• They devised a solar calendar and divided the year into 365 days with 12 months.

| priestly roles   large observatories |
| map the sky   astronomical phenomena   essential information |

Unit 10 55

Reading Comprehension

Main Idea

1. **What is the main idea of the passage?**

   a. Astronomy and agriculture are linked to one another.
   b. Ancient Chinese astronomers were the first to observe Halley's Comet.
   c. Modern technology allows astronomers to make detailed maps of the sky.
   d. Despite lacking modern technology, ancient astronomers still studied the stars.

Details

2. **What does them in the first paragraph refer to?**

   a. waves   b. astronomers   c. telescopes   d. images

3. **Why do modern astronomers rarely look through telescopes?**

   Because modern telescopes _____

4. **According to the passage, which of the following is NOT true?**

   a. The Chinese recorded and cataloged the stars.
   b. Ancient Egyptian astronomers built observatories.
   c. The locations of the pyramids were related to the stars.
   d. Astronomers use several waves to build pictures of the stars.

5. **What astronomical phenomena did the Chinese observe?**

   _____

6. **How were astronomy and agriculture linked in ancient Egypt?**

   a. Astronomers predicted the flooding of the Nile.
   b. Farmers divided the sky into five constellations.
   c. Calendars were produced based on growing seasons.
   d. Farmers studied the stars to know when to harvest crops.

Inference

7. **What CANNOT be inferred from the passage?**

   a. Humans have always been interested in the stars.
   b. Chinese astronomers accurately predicted rainy seasons.
   c. The Chinese mapped the constellations in the night sky.
   d. The Nile was a major water source for Egyptian farmers.

56   Chapter 5

Summary

Use the phrases in the box to complete the summary.

| devised calendars | pictures of the planets |
| locations of the pyramids | special buildings | the Nile River |

Astronomers today use advanced technology to study the stars. They use radio, infrared, X-ray, and gamma ray waves to build ❶_____. Ancient astronomers in Egypt and China also looked at and mapped the stars. However, they lacked modern technology. Chinese astronomers constructed ❷_____ from which they would study the stars. They recorded exploding stars, solar eclipses, and comets. In Egypt, astronomers played a priestly role in society. They would predict on what date ❸_____ would flood. They would then give the information to Egypt's farmers. Ancient Egyptian astronomers ❹_____ similar to our own. The ❺_____ reflected the constellations they saw in the night sky.

Language Focus

prepositions + which

You can use prepositions either before *which* (more formal) or at the end of relative clauses (more informal). We don't use *that* after prepositions.

EX *Astronomers were expected to predict the date **on which** the Nile River would flood. (O)*
*Astronomers were expected to predict the date **which** the Nile River would flood **on**. (O)*
*Astronomers were expected to predict the date **on that** the Nile River would flood. (X)*

Rewrite the sentences by using *prepositions + which*.

1. The valley which the town lies in is heavily polluted.
   ▸ _____

2. There are a number of safety procedures which you should be aware of.
   ▸ _____

3. Details are in the instruction manual which the camera was supplied with.
   ▸ _____

Chapter 6
Business & Marketing

Unit 11 Advertising in the Internet Age

Reading Skill | *Main Idea*
Language Focus | *too + adjective/adverb + to-infinitive*

Unit 12 Customized Online Ads

Reading Skill | *Cause & Effect*
Language Focus | *the emphatic "do"*

Unit 11

Just like the Internet has changed and developed over the years, Internet advertising has also changed over time. When you use the Internet, what types of advertisements do you see? Do you ever click on the advertisements or do you usually ignore them?

Unit 12

One way that Internet companies work to make their advertisements more effective is through the use of customized online ads. These are ads that try to promote specific products to each user. How do you think customized advertisements work? Why do you think they can be more effective than normal Internet ads?

Advertising in the Internet Age

Unit 11

▶ As you read, pay attention to how companies encourage people to click on Internet advertisements.

For most of the 20th century, advertising was simpler. Companies would create 30-second **jingles** for the radio. Or they would make minute-long ads for one of the three main television channels. Either strategy allowed them to reach millions of **potential** customers. Then the Internet came along. The Internet is different from previous media formats. It allows users to control the content they see. In this environment, how can advertising companies reach their audiences?

Currently, over 80 percent of advertising **budgets** are used for traditional media advertising. This includes ads for radio, newspapers, magazines, and television. Even so, Internet advertising is crucially important for most companies. Companies spend over $100 billion globally each year on Internet advertising, and this figure continues to rise. In the early days of the Internet, most ads were in the form of pop ups and **banner ads**. Today, browsers usually block pop ups automatically, and most users ignore banner ads. One research group found that these ads had a click-through rate of just 0.06 percent. Obviously, this number is far too low for companies and websites to make much profit on their advertising.

To make online advertising successful, many marketing firms are creating ways to **integrate** it into a website's content. Many websites today use news feeds to provide content. Internet companies **embed** advertisements in these lists of news stories and events to promote different companies' products. Think of how Facebook shows status updates from your friends. Or how Twitter shows a continually updated list of tweets. Along with seeing posts from your friends, you will often see advertisements. These ads are more effective because they are integrated into the content you wish to see.

Internet advertising will likely become even more widespread in the future. Companies will need to create more effective ads in order to continue providing free content and web services. **Words 308**

Vocabulary in Context

A Match the words or phrases in bold from the passage with their correct definitions.

1. _____ possible or likely to be
2. _____ to combine from multiple parts into one
3. _____ to insert something into another, larger thing
4. _____ a short, catchy song that is used in an advertisement
5. _____ an advertisement that appears at the top of a webpage
6. _____ the amount of money expected to be needed to do something

B Look at the underlined words in the passage and answer the questions.

1. The word "strategy" in the first paragraph is closest in meaning to _____.
   a. development   b. similarity   c. approach   d. shortage

2. The word "ignore" in the second paragraph is closest in meaning to _____.
   a. attend   b. disrespect   c. warn   d. neglect

3. The word "widespread" in the fourth paragraph is closest in meaning to _____.
   a. limited   b. regular   c. concentrated   d. popular

Reading Skill

The main idea of each paragraph gives a general idea that is explained in the rest of the paragraph.

Fill in the chart with the phrases in the box.

Paragraph 1	Companies are working to come up with new ways for ❶_____ to see advertisements online since people can ❷_____ they see.
Paragraph 2	Although Internet advertising makes up only 20 percent of ❸_____, it is becoming increasingly important for companies.
Paragraph 3	Advertisers are working on ways to ❹_____ into online content to make them more successful.

control the content   advertising budgets
potential customers   integrate advertisements

Reading Comprehension

Main Idea

1. **What is the passage mainly about?**

   a. the most successful companies that advertise online

   b. reasons that Internet users no longer click on pop up advertisements

   c. strategies companies use to make Internet advertising more effective

   d. how Facebook and Twitter are blocking advertisements from their sites

Details

2. **What does them in the first paragraph refer to?**

   a. television channels   b. companies   c. minute-long ads   d. jingles

3. **How is the Internet unlike earlier formats of media?**

   It is different because _____.

4. **According to the passage, which of the following is NOT true?**

   a. Very few people click on pop ups and banner ads anymore.

   b. Advertisements appear alongside a person's post on Twitter.

   c. Companies spend most of their money on traditional advertising.

   d. More than $100 billion is spent on traditional advertising each year.

5. **What are the formats of traditional media advertising?**

   _____

6. **Why are embedded advertisements more effective?**

   a. Because they are based on your interests

   b. Because they appear at the top of a webpage

   c. Because they are usually suggested by friends

   d. Because they are mixed in with the content you want to see

Inference

7. **What can be inferred from the passage?**

   a. Online advertising budgets will continue to increase in the future.

   b. Pop up advertisements are generally more effective than banner ads.

   c. Most people do not notice advertisements embedded in news feeds.

   d. Facebook and Twitter news feeds mainly consist of advertisements.

62   Chapter 6

Summary

Use the phrases in the box to complete the summary.

control over   alongside posts
advertising budgets   embedding advertisements   website's content

Advertising in the Internet age is important for companies. While 80 percent of ❶_____ are used for traditional media advertising, companies still spend more than $100 billion a year on Internet ads. However, because Internet users have total ❷_____ the content they see online, pop ups and banner ads are not very effective ways to advertise online. In response, companies are working to better integrate advertisements into a ❸_____. One of the ways they do this is by ❹_____ into news feeds online. When people use Facebook or Twitter, they will often see advertisements ❺_____ from their friends. These types of ads can be more effective since they are integrated into the content people wish to see online.

Language Focus

---
too + adjective/adverb + *to*-infinitive

To mean "more than necessary, possible, etc." to do something.

EX This number is very low. Websites cannot make much profit on their advertising.
    = This number is **too low** for websites **to make** much profit on their advertising.

Combine two sentences into one like the example in the box.

1. They arrived very late. They could not get seats.
   ➤ _____

2. There are so many people here. I cannot talk to all of them.
   ➤ _____

3. The suitcase was very small. He could not get all his clothes in.
   ➤ _____

Unit 11 63

Customized Online Ads

Unit 12

▶ *As you read, try to understand how companies gather information to create customized ads.*

Billions of people use search engines such as Google and Yahoo. Whenever you search for something, you see customized advertisements next to the search results. Internet companies **contend** that customized ads **make for** a better browsing experience. This may be true. However, **customized** ads do come with some drawbacks.

Many websites display customized advertisements based on many factors. These include the websites you have visited, the key words you have searched for, and your location. Using this information, Internet companies are able to show ads that are more **relevant** to each user. For example, suppose someone often visits cooking websites and watches instructional cooking videos online. This person will likely see ads for cooking products. At the same time, businesses, ranging from international corporations to locally owned shops, can earn more money. Furthermore, the website companies are able to provide content to their users for free because businesses pay the companies to advertise their products.

Internet companies claim they do not share their users' personal information with advertising companies. Even so, many have concerns about users' privacy. Whenever someone visits almost any website, a small **packet** of data is downloaded to the person's browser. This is called a cookie. The cookie tracks people's search preferences on their computer. Companies use this information to create customized ads. Some feel that this is a violation of personal privacy. Others worry that cookies could install viruses on their computers. In reality, cookies are text files that can only be read by the websites that send them to your computer.

For those concerned about privacy, there are some solutions. Many websites offer an option to **opt out of** personalized ads. Most web browsers have a security option to disable cookies for further privacy. However, there is still no way to block all ads from every website. It seems that users have to deal with advertisements along with their Internet experience.

Words 316

64 Chapter 6

Vocabulary in Context

A **Match the words or phrases in bold from the passage with their correct definitions.**

1. _____ related to the topic
2. _____ to choose not to do something
3. _____ to allow or cause something to happen
4. _____ to argue or believe something to be true
5. _____ computer information in small amounts
6. _____ to change something to how you want it to be

B **Look at the underlined words in the passage and answer the questions.**

1. The word "drawback" in the first paragraph is closest in meaning to _____.
   a. benefit   b. evidence   c. disadvantage   d. indication

2. The word "track" in the third paragraph is closest in meaning to _____.
   a. restrict   b. monitor   c. share   d. alter

3. The word "disable" in the fourth paragraph is closest in meaning to _____.
   a. deactivate   b. attack   c. permit   d. integrate

Reading Skill *Cause and effect is when one event causes something to happen. The cause explains why something happens, and the effect is what happens as a result.*

Fill in the chart with the phrases in the box.

Cause	Effect
Websites track which websites users visit, the key words they search for, and their location.	Companies are able to show ads that are ❶_____ to each user.
A person likes to visit cooking websites and often watches cooking videos online.	This person will probably ❷_____ for cooking products.
Whenever you visit a website, a small ❸_____ called a cookie is downloaded to your computer.	The cookie tracks your ❹_____ to generate customized advertisements.

| see ads | packet of information | more relevant | search preferences |

Reading Comprehension

Main Idea

1 **What is the best title for the passage?**

   a. Tips for Staying Safe on the Internet

   b. The Benefits and Drawbacks of Customized Ads

   c. How Cookies Are Harming People's Privacy Online

   d. How Websites Are Trying to Improve Their Services

Details

2 **What do search websites argue in favor of customized ads next to search results?**

   _____

3 **According to the passage, which of the following is true?**

   a. Customized ads differ based on where a person lives.

   b. Most Internet ads are made by international businesses.

   c. Cookies sometimes install viruses on people's computers.

   d. Many companies share people's personal information with advertisers.

4 **What does this information in the third paragraph refer to?**

   a. Internet cookies

   b. the person's browser

   c. users' personal information

   d. people's search preferences

5 **Why do some users think that personalized ads violate their privacy?**

   _____

6 **What can users do to see fewer personalized ads?**

   a. change Internet browsers

   b. pay websites to take down the ads

   c. disable cookies in their web browser

   d. use different key words in their searches

Inference

7 **What CANNOT be inferred from the passage?**

   a. Internet ads are used to cover the costs of operating websites.

   b. Local businesses rely on Internet ads more than large companies do.

   c. Personalized ads can be more effective than random advertisements.

   d. Some ads will still pop up even if people disable cookies in their browsers.

Summary

Use the phrases in the box to complete the summary.

| key words | provide free content |
| users' privacy | from cookies | some drawbacks |

Whenever you use search engines such as Google, you see customized advertisements next to the search results. These advertisements have some advantages but also ❶_____. Customized advertisements are created based on what websites you have visited, what ❷_____ you have searched for, and so forth. This information allows companies to create more relevant ads for each user. As a result, companies can make more money while websites use the money from advertisements to ❸_____. However, some worry about ❹_____. Personalized ads are created using the information ❺_____ on websites. Some feel that creating ads from this information is a violation of privacy. Luckily, there are ways for users to block personalized ads. Even so, it is not possible to block all the ads we see online.

Language Focus

> **the emphatic *do***
>
> *Do* can be used to emphasize an affirmative verb. *Does* is used for the third person and *did* is used for the past tense.
>
> EX *Customized ads <u>come</u> with some drawbacks.*
> → *Customized ads **do come** with some drawbacks.*

Rewrite the sentences to emphasize the underlined verbs.

1. She <u>looks</u> so beautiful in her wedding dress.
   ➤ _____

2. My memory isn't very good, but I <u>remember</u> what she was wearing.
   ➤ _____

3. I don't get much exercise now, but I <u>played</u> football a lot when I was younger.
   ➤ _____

Unit 12

Chapter 7
Animals

Unit 13 Why Can't Ostriches Fly?

Reading Skill | *Main Idea & Details*
Language Focus | *no ~ as + adjective/adverb + as*

Unit 14 The Swimming Nose

Reading Skill | *Main Idea*
Language Focus | *high vs. highly*

Unit 13

Ostriches are the largest bird. They can weigh 120 kilograms or more and be taller than a grown man. Despite their size and power, ostriches cannot fly. Why do you think ostriches are unable to fly? How do you think ostriches keep themselves safe even though they cannot fly?

Unit 14

Many people consider sharks to be dangerous animals to human beings. Do you think sharks are as dangerous as people believe? Do you think human beings ever treat sharks badly? What can we do to better understand sharks?

Why Can't Ostriches Fly?

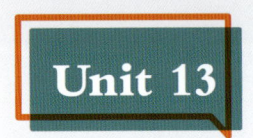

▶ As you read, pay attention to the reasons that ostriches cannot fly.

Ostriches are the largest and fastest birds in the world. However, there is one area in which ostriches will never compete with other birds: Ostriches cannot fly.

Ostriches **outclass** nearly all other birds in many ways. They have a strong, feathery **rump** of a body, a long neck, and a sharp **beak**. Ostriches are also equipped with the biggest eyeballs of any bird, measuring five centimeters across. No other bird can run as fast as an ostrich. They can cover the *savannas of Africa at over 60 kilometers per hour. They can survive in the desert, grow to 2.5 meters in height, and live to be forty years old. Being formidable defenders of themselves from potential **predators**, they have claws on their feet that can seriously harm any opponent.

Even so, ostriches cannot fly because of their physical **attributes**. Flying birds have a keel, which is the bone that is attached to the muscles that move a bird's wings, but ostriches lack one. Birds that can fly also have a rounded breastbone while the ostrich's breastbone is flat. Furthermore, the wings of an ostrich are short and incapable of flight. Like other flightless birds, ostriches also tend to have more feathers than those that can fly. So, although it is a bird, the ostrich will never be able to take off the land.

It is not just the ostrich that cannot fly. Eighteen species of penguins, a single parrot species, and the emu are also flightless. Often found on islands, birds that lost the need for flight lost the power of flight. Predators that they would formerly have flown away from to escape disappeared from their environment. Without this **stimulus**, these birds gradually lost their ability to fly.

Although ostriches are superior to other birds in many ways, they will never be able to take to the skies.   Words 308

*savanna: a large, flat grassy area where wild animals live, especially in Africa

Vocabulary in Context

A Match the words in bold from the passage with their correct definitions.

1. _____ to be superior to others
2. _____ the rear part of an animal's body
3. _____ a feature or characteristic of something
4. _____ an animal that kills other animals for food
5. _____ something that causes a change or reaction
6. _____ the hard pointed part covering a bird's mouth

B Look at the underlined words in the passage and answer the questions.

1. The word "compete" in the first paragraph is closest in meaning to _____.
   a. waste   b. resume   c. contest   d. block

2. The word "formidable" in the second paragraph is closest in meaning to _____.
   a. pleasant   b. powerful   c. discouraging   d. confident

3. The word "opponent" in the second paragraph is closest in meaning to _____.
   a. supporter   b. challenger   c. expert   d. partner

Reading Skill *The main idea is usually at the beginning of a text and makes a general statement. The supporting details are specific ideas that support the main idea.*

Fill in the chart with the phrases in the box.

Paragraph 2	Ostriches are ❶_____ other birds in many ways. • They have a strong body, can run over 60 kilometers per hour, and grow to be 2.5 meters tall.
Paragraph 3	Ostriches cannot fly because of their ❷_____. • Ostriches have a ❸_____, whereas flying birds have a rounded one. • Their wings are too short for them to fly and they lack a keel.
Paragraph 4	Many flightless birds cannot fly because they lost the ❹_____. • Predators that they would have flown away from disappeared from their environment.

flat breastbone	power of flight	superior to	physical characteristics

Reading Comprehension

Main Idea

1. **What is the main idea of the passage?**

    a. Predators hunt flightless birds very easily.

    b. Flightless birds share certain characteristics.

    c. The ostrich is a large bird that is unable to fly.

    d. The natural environment of island birds is changing.

Details

2. **How does an ostrich defend itself against predators?**

   _____

3. **What does one in the third paragraph refer to?**

    a. muscle   b. keel   c. wing   d. attribute

4. **According to the passage, which of the following is NOT true?**

    a. Ostriches have the largest eyeballs of all birds.

    b. Ostriches can run faster than any other bird.

    c. Ostriches can grow to be very large and live for a decade.

    d. Some species of penguins and a parrot species are flightless.

5. **What is not mentioned as a difference between ostriches and flying birds?**

    a. Ostriches have a flat breastbone.

    b. Ostriches have a large keel bone.

    c. The wings of an ostrich are short.

    d. Ostriches have more feathers than flying birds.

6. **Why did some birds lose the ability to fly?**

   _____

Inference

7. **What CANNOT be inferred from the passage?**

    a. Some flightless birds once flew in the sky.

    b. Birds use flight to escape from predators.

    c. Birds with a lot of feathers are better at flying.

    d. The keel bone is small or missing in eighteen species of penguins.

72 Chapter 7

Summary

Use the phrases in the box to complete the summary.

| short wings | claws on their feet |
| more feathers | disappeared from | the keel bone |

Ostriches are large birds. They are the fastest and heaviest in the world. They can survive in the desert and defend themselves well against predators with the ❶_____. Despite these advantages, ostriches cannot fly. The ostrich cannot fly because it is missing ❷_____. This bone supports the muscles that allow a bird to fly. Ostriches also have flat breastbones and ❸_____. At the same time, ostriches have ❹_____ than birds that can fly. Other flightless birds include some penguins, the emu, and one species of parrot. Often, birds became flightless because predators they would have flown away from to escape ❺_____ their environment.

Language Focus

no ~ as + adjective/adverb + as

We can express the same idea using different forms of the same adjective or adverb, the positive, the comparative and the superlative.

EX **No** other bird can run **as fast as** an ostrich.
= An ostrich can run **faster than** any other bird.
= An ostrich can run the **fastest** of all the birds.

Rewrite the sentences by using superlatives.

1. No other rock flew as high as my rock.

   ▶ _____

2. No other thing in the world is as important as love.

   ▶ _____

3. The Atacama Desert is drier than any other place on Earth.

   ▶ _____

The Swimming Nose

Unit 14

▸ *While you read, try to understand the threats to sharks and what their characteristics are.*

People think of a shark as a blue triangular **fin** cutting through the ocean surface. They think a shark is always looking for something to kill and eat. The shark's nickname the "swimming nose" reflects people's tendency to see it only as a dangerous predator. While sharks are responsible for the deaths of an average of six humans each year, bees and wasps are responsible for about a hundred. This is just one of the **misconceptions** people have about this intelligent animal of the deep.

Contrary to their image as a scary predator, thousands of sharks are hunted and killed each year for products that can be produced from their skins. Sharkskin is covered with tiny teeth-like objects called denticles. In Japan and Germany, sharkskin was used to make sword handles because its nonslip surface provided a good **grip**. Sharkskin was also used as sandpaper to smooth out rough surfaces and is used as a leather to make durable shoes. Sharks are also hunted for their liver oil, which is rich in vitamin A, even though a method has been devised synthetically to produce it.

▲ shark liver oil capsules

Scientists have been working to understand sharks better. Researchers **submerge** themselves underwater to **undertake** close-up research on sharks. They describe the predator as intelligent. They have also discovered that sharks have astonishing senses. The 400-million-year-old animal is highly **adept** at detecting the nearness of other fish. Sharks can hear the sounds and movements of fish that are hundreds of meters away and can detect the nearness of fish at night. They even know when fish are hiding in sand. Combined with the 30 to 60 kilometers per hour a shark can move at, its sensory skills make it a formidable animal. Yet it is not always looking for food. The great white shark can go over three months without eating.

Sharks may be intimidating animals, but they are also intelligent creatures that we should protect.

Words 320

Vocabulary in Context

A Match the words in bold from the passage with their correct definitions.

1. _____ to go below the surface of water
2. _____ a mistaken belief about something
3. _____ the act of holding something very tightly
4. _____ to begin doing a long or difficult activity
5. _____ good at doing something quite difficult
6. _____ a thin, triangular part on a fish, which helps it to swim

B Look at the underlined words in the passage and answer the questions.

1. The word "synthetically" in the second paragraph is closest in meaning to _____.
   a. silently   b. generally   c. naturally   d. artificially

2. The word "detect" in the third paragraph is closest in meaning to _____.
   a. watch   b. hide   c. notice   d. reveal

3. The word "intimidating" in the fourth paragraph is closest in meaning to _____.
   a. terrific   b. frightening   c. comforting   d. convenient

Reading Skill The main idea of each paragraph gives a general idea that is explained in the rest of the paragraph.

Fill in the chart with the phrases in the box.

Paragraph 1	People consider the shark ❶_____, but ❷_____ kill more people each year than sharks.
Paragraph 2	Each year, people kill ❸_____ to make products from their skin.
Paragraph 3	Researchers have been working to understand sharks better by ❹_____.

bees or wasps	a dangerous predator
studying them underwater	thousands of sharks

Unit 14 75

Reading Comprehension

Main Idea

1. **What is the main idea of the passage?**

   a. Sharks are largely misunderstood creatures.
   b. Sharks have the best senses of any sea creature.
   c. Most beliefs about sharks are supported by research.
   d. Thousands of sharks are killed each year for their skins.

Details

2. **What is one of the misconceptions people have about sharks?**

   _____

3. **What does it in the second paragraph refer to?**

   a. vitamin A   b. a denticle   c. sharkskin   d. liver oil

4. **According to the passage, which of the following is NOT true?**

   a. Shark liver oil is rich in vitamin A.
   b. About a hundred people are killed by sharks each year.
   c. Researchers study sharks underwater for close-up research.
   d. Sharks' skin is used to make some products because it has denticles.

5. **Why was sharkskin used to make sword handles?**

   _____

6. **Which of the following is NOT true about sharks?**

   a. Their senses are poor during nighttime.
   b. They know when fish are hiding in sand.
   c. They can hear animals that are hundreds of meters away.
   d. The great white sharks are able to survive for three months without food.

Inference

7. **What can be inferred from the passage?**

   a. Sharks primarily use their hearing to hunt.
   b. More people were attacked by sharks in the past.
   c. People no longer make products from sharkskin.
   d. Modern sharks are different from sharks millions of years ago.

Summary

Use the phrases in the box to complete the summary.

| during the nighttime | skins and organs |
| shark liver oil | tiny teeth-like objects | well-developed senses |

Sharks are not as dangerous as people think. They are only responsible for around six human deaths each year, while bees and wasps kill about a hundred people. Sharks are hunted by humans, who make different products from their ❶_____. Sharkskin is covered with ❷_____ called denticles and can be used to make sandpaper, shoes, and handles. ❸_____ is produced because of its richness in vitamin A. Researchers describe sharks as intelligent and having ❹_____. They can detect other fish in the sea that are far away. They can also detect them ❺_____ and when they are in sand. The shark is a formidable animal.

Language Focus

> **high vs. highly**
>
> *High* refers to height. *Highly* expresses an extreme degree, meaning "very much."
>
> EX *She stretched her arms up **high**.*
> *Sharks are **highly** adept at detecting the nearness of other fish.*

Read each sentence and choose the correct word.

1. He kicked the ball (high / highly) over the goal.
2. We could just see the plane flying (high / highly) overhead.
3. It's (high / highly) unlikely that the construction will be finished on time.
4. She is one of the most (high / highly) regarded researchers in the university.

Chapter 8
History & Origins

Unit 15 The First Modern Olympics

Reading Skill | *Sequencing*
Language Focus | *It is[was] ~ that*

Unit 16 Calendar Systems of the World

Reading Skill | *Categorizing*
Language Focus | *conjunction (+ subject + be)*

Unit 15

The Olympic Games date back to ancient Greece. In 1896, the first modern Olympic Games were held. Today, the Olympics are one of the most significant sports events in the world. What do you think the main purpose of the Olympics is? Do you think the Olympics should continue to be held?

Unit 16

If you ask most people about the calendar, they will say that it has 12 months and 365 days a year. That is the system used by the Gregorian calendar, which is just one of many calendar systems used throughout history. Do you know of any other calendar systems? How might they be different from the Gregorian calendar?

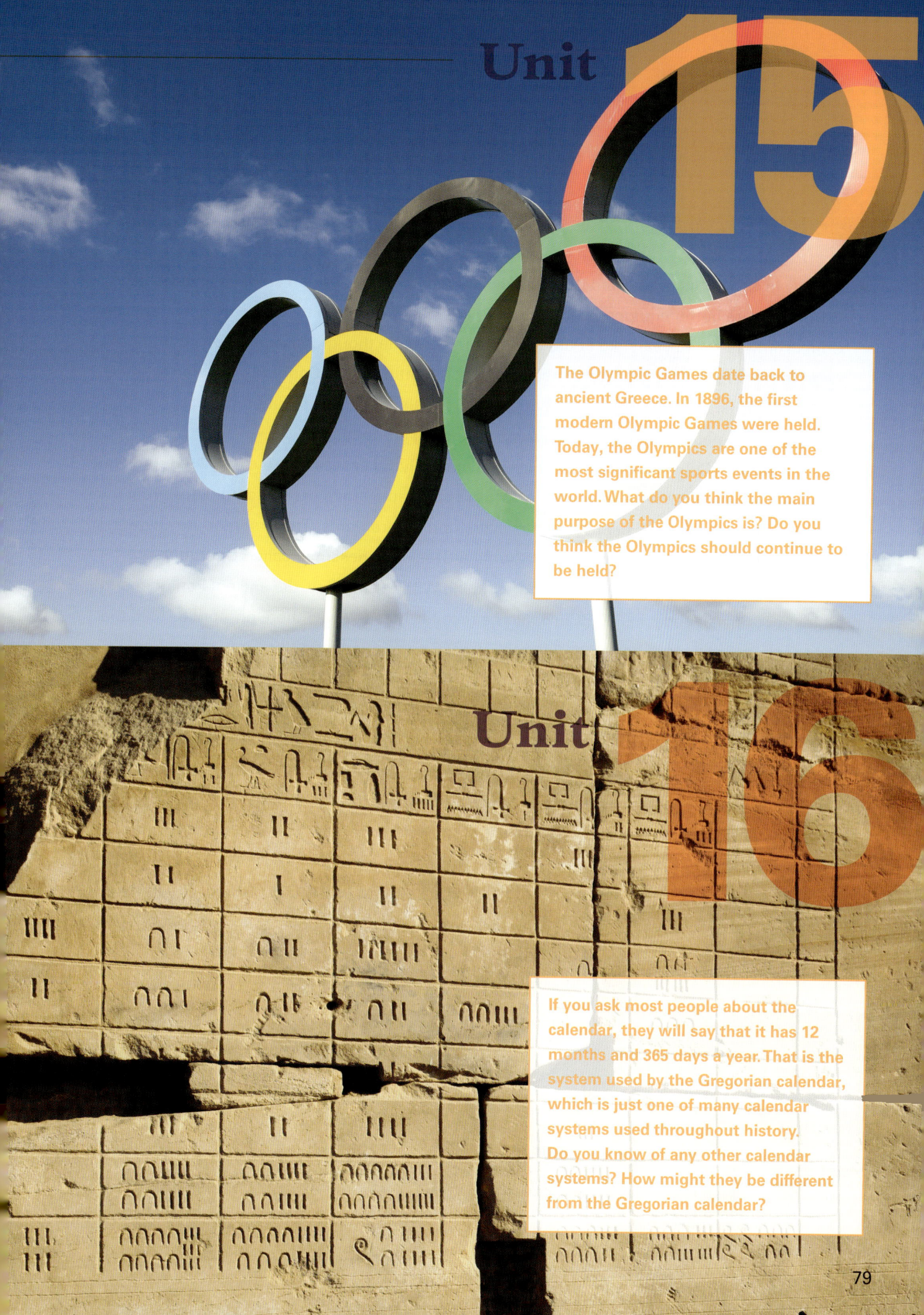

The First Modern Olympics

Unit 15

▶ As you read, consider why the Olympic Games were brought back and how the event was organized.

In 1870, France suffered defeat and occupation when German soldiers invaded. The Germans were better equipped and organized and easily **overran** their opponents. Pierre de Coubertin was seven years old at the time. As an adult, he thought his country's youth needed **reinvigorating** and that the world needed to stop fighting wars. Coubertin decided that the revival of the ancient Olympic Games could improve the physical condition of Europe's youth while bringing nations together in a peaceful sporting competition.

In 1894, Coubertin's campaign for a revived Olympics was approved by 79 **delegates** from nine countries. It was the French **aristocrat** and educator's dream to hold the event in its ancient home of Athens. There were, however, funding problems. The first modern Olympics almost got moved to Budapest, Hungary, until a Greek businessman called George Averoff **stepped in** and contributed a million *drachmas. With this money, the ancient Panathenaic Stadium, originally built in 330 BCE, could be reconstructed. It was there on April 6, 1896 that King George I of Greece declared, "I hereby proclaim the opening of the First International Olympic Games at Athens."

Only fourteen countries competed in 43 events. Most of the athletes were Greek. **Some** were even tourists vacationing in Greece at the time of the games. Competitors wore their own clothing and had little financial support from their national governments. The events of the games are recognizable today. There were track and field events, weightlifting, swimming, and shooting, amongst others. The highlight of the games was the marathon. It was run from the town of Marathon to Athens. This was the same route run by a Greek soldier, who was delivering news of a Greek victory over their Persian enemy, in 490 BCE. Greeks cheered again in 1896 as their **countryman**, Spiridon Louis, entered the Panathenaic Stadium first to win the race. **Words 306**

*drachma: the currency in Greece before the adoption of the Euro in 2002

▼ Panathenaic Stadium in Athens

Vocabulary in Context

A **Match the words or phrases in bold from the passage with their correct definitions.**

1. _____ to defeat quickly and easily
2. _____ a person from the same country as you
3. _____ to give energy and power back to something
4. _____ a person born into a rich, upper-class family
5. _____ a representative for a country or business at an event
6. _____ to become involved in a difficult situation to provide help

B **Look at the underlined words in the passage and answer the questions.**

1. The word "approve" in the second paragraph is closest in meaning to _____.
   a. accept   b. deny   c. obtain   d. outline

2. The word "declare" in the second paragraph is closest in meaning to _____.
   a. confuse   b. seek   c. announce   d. recommend

3. The word "recognizable" in the third paragraph is closest in meaning to _____.
   a. preferable   b. noticeable   c. excellent   d. astonishing

Reading Skill *Sequencing is putting events in order from first to last. When we sequence, we can easily understand which events happen first, second, and so on.*

Fill in the chart and number the events in order.

	❶_____ Coubertin decided to revive the Olympic Games of ancient Greece.
	Spiridon Louis entered the Panathenaic Stadium first to ❷_____.
	❸_____ provided one million drachmas to help pay for the games.
	Germany ❹_____ and easily defeated their opponents.
	The games opened with competitors from ❺_____ participating in 43 events.

French aristocrat   14 countries
invaded France   win the marathon   a Greek businessman

Unit 15 81

Reading Comprehension

Main Idea

1 **What is the main idea of the passage?**

   a. The first modern Olympics were not very successful.

   b. Pierre de Coubertin was a critic of the Olympic Games.

   c. The Olympics were brought back because of one man's dream.

   d. The events at the first Olympics were different from the ones of today.

Details

2 **According to the passage, which of the following is NOT true?**

   a. King George I opened the first Olympic Games.

   b. George Averoff helped to fund the 1896 Olympics.

   c. Pierre de Coubertin wanted to stop people from fighting wars.

   d. Representatives from 79 countries approved the Olympic revival.

3 **Why were the games nearly held in Budapest?**

_____

4 **What does Some in the third paragraph refer to?**

   a. some games   b. some athletes   c. some countries   d. some events

5 **Which of the following is true about the 1896 Olympics?**

   a. Athletes from 43 countries competed.

   b. The winner of the marathon was a Greek soldier.

   c. All the competitors were sponsored by their home nations.

   d. The events from those games are still held in today's Olympics.

6 **What was significant about the route of the marathon in the first Olympics?**

_____

Inference

7 **What CANNOT be inferred from the passage?**

   a. The Olympic Games are an historic event.

   b. Greek athletes regularly win the marathon at the Olympics.

   c. The German army was stronger than the French army in 1870.

   d. The Olympic Games might not exist if it had not been for Pierre de Coubertin.

Summary

Use the phrases in the box to complete the summary.

	German army	held in Greece
fighting wars	over forty events	revive the Olympics

France was invaded and easily defeated by the ❶_____ in 1870. A Frenchman named Pierre de Coubertin decided that his country's youth required more physical exercise and that nations should stop ❷_____ against each other. He decided to ❸_____. The first modern Olympics were ❹_____ in 1896. A Greek businessman paid for the reconstruction of an ancient stadium. Only fourteen countries competed. However, there were ❺_____, including weightlifting, swimming, and shooting. The highlight was the marathon. It was run from the Greek town of Marathon itself. Greeks cheered as one of their countrymen entered the reconstructed but ancient stadium first.

Language Focus

> **It is[was] ~ that**
>
> *It* can be used with *that*-clauses to emphasize one part of a sentence. *Who* is possible instead of *that* when a personal subject is emphasized.
>
> EX **It was** there on April 6, 1896 **that** King George I of Greece declared, "I hereby proclaim the opening of the First International Olympic Games at Athens."

Rewrite the sentences to emphasize the underlined information.

1. My uncle took Peter to New York yesterday.
   ▶ _____

2. Alexander Graham Bell invented the telephone in 1876.
   ▶ _____

3. His attitude towards other people really annoys me.
   ▶ _____

Calendar Systems of the World

Unit 16

▶ While reading, pay attention to how the calendar systems are unique and how they are similar.

"What's today's date?" This **straightforward** question seems to have a straightforward answer. In truth, over 40 different calendars are used all over the world today, and they all have different systems for determining the date, month, and even the year.

One of the oldest known calendars is the Mayan calendar, which uses two systems to calculate the date. The first is the *Tzolkin* calendar. It has a 260-day cycle. The second is the 365-day solar cycle called the *Haab'*. These calendars do not have an indication for years. However, when combined, the dates of the *Tzolkin* and *Haab'* calendars can specify a unique day within a 52-year cycle called a Calendar Round. This calendar is still used by some people living in Guatemala.

▲ the Mayan calendar

In East Asia, the Chinese lunar calendar remains influential. Each lunar New Year in the Chinese calendar usually starts between January 20th and February 20th, about one month after the start of the Chinese solar year. Common years are 12 months long, with **leap years** having 13 of them. While no longer the official calendar, the Chinese calendar is still used in China to celebrate traditional holidays. It is also used to choose **auspicious** days to have weddings, move home, or start a business. People in countries influenced by China, including Vietnam, Korea, and Japan, use the Chinese calendar for the same reasons.

The most widely used calendar in the world today is the Gregorian calendar. It was introduced in the 16th century by Pope Gregory XIII as a **modification** to the Julian calendar. Each year in the Gregorian calendar is divided into 12 months of 365 days. The exception is the leap year, which has 366 days and occurs every four years. This extra day is added to keep the date of the calendar more **in line with** the movement of the sun. In the late 19th century, most countries **adopted** it for international business purposes.

Words 320

Vocabulary in Context

A Match the words or phrases in bold from the passage with their correct definitions.

1. _____ a change or adjustment
2. _____ to begin using something
3. _____ simple to understand; direct
4. _____ in the same position as something else
5. _____ a year that has an extra day or extra month
6. _____ indicating or suggesting that future success is likely

B Look at the underlined words in the passage and answer the questions.

1. The word "determine" in the first paragraph is closest in meaning to _____.
   a. fix   b. decide   c. argue   d. create

2. The word "indication" in the second paragraph is closest in meaning to _____.
   a. sign   b. construction   c. statue   d. hint

3. The word "influential" in the third paragraph is closest in meaning to _____.
   a. inactive   b. confusing   c. promising   d. significant

Reading Skill *Categorizing information means to arrange information or items into different groups.*

Fill in the chart with the phrases in the box.

Mayan Calendar	• uses two separate calendar systems, the *Tzolkin* and *Haab'* • has no indication for years, but can specify ❶_____ by using the Calendar Round, which is still used by some people ❷_____
Chinese Lunar Calendar	• Chinese Lunar New Year starts about one month after the solar year. • has common years with 12 months, ❸_____ with 13 months • is still used to plan ❹_____
Gregorian Calendar	• was introduced as a modification to the ❺_____ • Each year has 12 months of 365 days, with a leap year of 366 days. • was adopted by most countries in the 19th century for business

leap years   a unique day   Julian calendar   in Guatemala   special events

Reading Comprehension

Main Idea

1 **What is the passage mainly about?**

　　a. ancient calendar systems that are no longer used
　　b. reasons why the Gregorian calendar became so widely used
　　c. why the Chinese calendar is still used by people in East Asia
　　d. various types of calendar systems used throughout the world

Details

2 **How did the Mayan calendar specify a unique date?**

_____

3 **What does them in the third paragraph refer to?**

　　a. months　　b. leap years　　c. common years　　d. holidays

4 **Who still uses the Mayan calendar?**

_____

5 **According to the passage, which of the following is true?**

　　a. The Mayan calendar includes an indication for the year.
　　b. The Julian calendar is based on the Gregorian calendar.
　　c. The Chinese Lunar New Year always starts on the same date.
　　d. East Asians sometimes use the Chinese lunar calendar to plan some special events.

6 **Why does the Gregorian calendar include a leap year?**

　　a. to help promote international business
　　b. to keep the date in line with the Julian calendar
　　c. to start the new year based on the Chinese calendar
　　d. to keep the date more accurate with the sun's movements

Inference

7 **What can be inferred from the passage?**

　　a. The actual solar year is longer than 365 days.
　　b. Most calendar systems were introduced by the Pope.
　　c. It is unusual for calendar systems to indicate the year.
　　d. Most Chinese people prefer using the Chinese lunar calendar.

Summary

Use the phrases in the box to complete the summary.

| the sun's movements | determine the date |
| 12 or 13 months | specify the year | lucky days |

Few people realize how many different calendar systems are used throughout the world. The Mayan calendar is one of the oldest known calendars. It uses two different calendars to ❶ _____. Although these calendars do not ❷ _____, when combined, they indicate a unique date within the 52-year Calendar Round. The Chinese lunar calendar remains important in East Asian countries. People in these countries use it to celebrate holidays and to choose ❸ _____ for various events. This calendar starts between January and February 20th and has either ❹ _____. The most widely used calendar in the world is the Gregorian calendar. It consists of 12 months of 365 days. Leap years have 366 days to keep the calendar more accurate with ❺ _____.

Language Focus

conjunction (+ subject + be)

Subject pronoun and the verb *be* can be omitted after while, when, etc.

EX While **(it is)** no longer the official calendar, the Chinese calendar is still used in China to celebrate traditional holidays.

Rewrite the sentences with a reduced clause like the example in the box.

1. Jim hurt his knee while he was playing tennis.

    ▶ _____

2. When you are in Madrid, you must visit the Prado Museum.

    ▶ _____

3. When they are combined, the dates of the *Tzolkin* and *Haab'* calendars can specify a unique day within a 52-year cycle.

    ▶ _____

Developing Background Knowledge and Reading Strategies

Reading

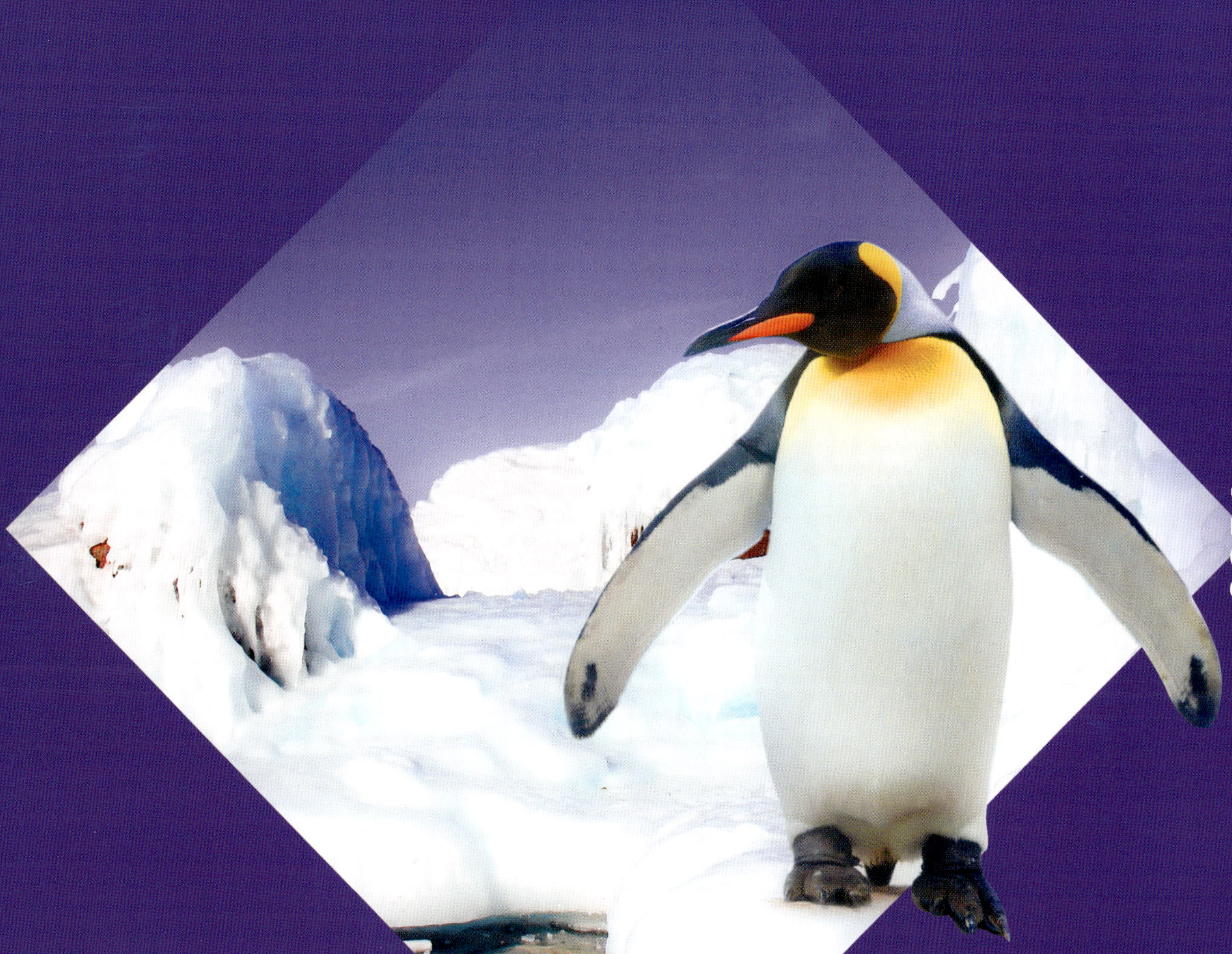

Voyage

3

PLUS

WORKBOOK

Reading Voyage 3

PLUS

WORKBOOK

Lake Baikal, the Blue Eye of Siberia

Vocabulary Practice

A Write each word or phrase next to its correct definition. Then write its meaning in your language.

exile	famed	reroute	crescent	sustain
vast	sediment	volume	shoreline	fresh water

1. famous or notable _____ _____
2. water that is not salty _____ _____
3. to keep up or maintain _____ _____
4. very large in size or amount _____ _____
5. material at the bottom of the water _____ _____
6. the amount of space that a liquid fills _____ _____
7. the land along the edge of a body of water _____ _____
8. someone who is forced to leave their country _____ _____
9. to change the direction or movement of something; to redirect _____ _____
10. a curved shape that is wide in the middle with two pointed ends _____ _____

B Use the words or phrases from A to complete the sentences. Change the forms if necessary.

1. This filter removes 99.9 percent of the _____ from your water.
2. The Sahara is a _____ desert located in the northern part of Africa.
3. There is not enough oxygen to _____ life at very high altitudes.
4. The moon is shaped like a _____ before and after the new moon.
5. Napoleon was forced to spend his final years as a political _____ on Saint Helena Island.

2

Writing Practice

C Circle the correct words and translate the sentences into your language.

1. It was not discovered (until / in) 1643 despite being 25 million years old.
   ➤ _____

2. An oil pipeline had to be rerouted away from Baikal (in spite of / because of) fears of possible oil spills.
   ➤ _____

3. One Siberian feature that is considered to be a natural wonder of the world (is / are) Lake Baikal.
   ➤ _____

4. (Situating / Situated) in the largest country in the world, Russia, the region of Siberia is vast.
   ➤ _____

More Reading Comprehension

D Read the passage and answer the questions.

> Lake Baikal is 31,500 square kilometers, (A) making it the seventh largest lake in the world by area. _____, it is the largest lake in the world by volume. The reason is it is the deepest lake in the world, extending down more than 1,600 meters at its maximum point of depth. It contains 20% of the world's fresh water that is not (B) frozen. Beneath its water is another 7 kilometers of sediment. This 600-kilometer-long crescent-shaped lake (C) sustains over 1,000 species of plants and animals that can (D) found nowhere else on the planet. The lake's largest island is 72 kilometers long, and over 300 streams and rivers flow into Baikal. It is a wonder of nature.

1. Which is the most appropriate for the blank?

   a. Otherwise   b. Even so   c. Thus   d. On the other hand

2. Which one is NOT grammatically correct in the passage?

   a. (A)   b. (B)   c. (C)   d. (D)

The Harbor of Rio De Janeiro

Vocabulary Practice

A Write each word next to its correct definition. Then write its meaning in your language.

| colony | settler | resemble | harbor | intervention |
| debase | recognition | hunchback | overlook | urbanization |

1. to look like something else   _____   _____
2. special attention given to an event   _____   _____
3. a person with an unusually curved spine   _____   _____
4. the act of becoming involved in an event   _____   _____
5. to have a view looking down at something   _____   _____
6. to make something worse or lower in quality   _____   _____
7. the first people who move to and live on a piece of land   _____   _____
8. the process of an area becoming more developed like a city   _____   _____
9. an area controlled by a country that is usually far away from it   _____   _____
10. a part of water that is next to land and is safe enough for ships to enter   _____   _____

B Use the words from A to complete the sentences. Change the forms if necessary.

1. A police _____ was needed to break up the fight.

2. As she got older, my grandmother started to look like a _____.

3. Sally won a medal in _____ for her community service work.

4. The Philippines was a _____ of the United States for many years.

5. Rural areas go through the process of _____ before turning into cities.

Writing Practice

C Circle the correct words and translate the sentences into your language.

1. Has it (enhanced / been enhanced) or debased by human intervention in nature?

   ➤ _____

2. Human intervention has already done (too much / too many) damage to this natural wonder.

   ➤ _____

3. Some estimate that 70 percent of Rio's sewage is dumped (direct / directly) into Guanabara Bay.

   ➤ _____

4. Natives had called the harbor Guanabara, (that / which) means "the arm of the sea."

   ➤ _____

More Reading Comprehension

D Read the passage and answer the questions.

> In 1555, the French established a colony (A) <u>on</u> one of the islands in the harbor. ⓐ Just a year later, they were kicked out (B) <u>by</u> Portuguese settlers. ⓑ It remained the capital of Brazil (C) <u>until</u> 1960 when the capital was changed to Brasilia. ⓒ Today, Rio de Janeiro is world famous (D) <u>of</u> its beautiful beaches and mountain cable cars. ⓓ The "hunchback" now carries a passenger: the statue of Christ the Redeemer. This 38-meter tall statue overlooks the harbor and is a symbol of Rio.

1. Which is the best place for the sentence?

   > They established the city of Rio de Janeiro.

   a. ⓐ b. ⓑ c. ⓒ d. ⓓ

2. Which one is NOT grammatically correct in the passage?

   a. (A) b. (B) c. (C) d. (D)

Unit 3 The Global Refugee Crisis

Vocabulary Practice

A Write each word or phrase next to its correct definition. Then write its meaning in your language.

| sanitation | uproot | disaster | flee | permanent |
| humanitarian | assist | persecution | relief | asylum seeker |

1. long lasting; forever _____ _____
2. to help someone to do something _____ _____
3. a huge event that causes a lot of damage _____ _____
4. to escape an area usually because of danger _____ _____
5. to leave a place where you have lived for a long time _____ _____
6. relating to work that helps people improve their lives _____ _____
7. aid or assistance given to people in difficult situations _____ _____
8. the process of providing cleaning services such as collecting garbage _____ _____
9. the act of treating people cruelly because of their beliefs _____ _____
10. a person seeking refugee status who hasn't get it yet _____ _____

B Use the words or phrases from A to complete the sentences. Change the forms if necessary.

1. You should always try to _____ a dangerous situation if possible.
2. Cities in ancient Rome provided _____ services such as trash removal.
3. The Red Cross is one of the largest _____ organizations in the world.
4. Thousands of citizens were _____ from their homes following the flood.
5. The government provided food, water, and other _____ items after the storm.

6

Writing Practice

C Circle the correct words and translate the sentences into your language.

1. We can have (regular / regularly) access to food and water.
   ▶ _____

2. (Due to / In spite of) natural disasters, these people have been uprooted from their homelands.
   ▶ _____

3. The United Nations Relief and Works Agency offers longer-term services (to / for) refugees.
   ▶ _____

4. The UN defines a refugee as someone who escapes to another country due to events that (disturbs / disturb) public order.
   ▶ _____

More Reading Comprehension

D Read the passage and answer the questions.

> The UN estimates that over 43 million people today are displaced. Around 15 million of these people are refugees. Another one million of them are asylum seekers. Asylum seekers differ from other types of refugees because <u>they</u> do not hold official refugee status yet. Among all refugees, the UN estimates that between 6 and 12 million are stateless. These people are not official citizens of any nation. _____, they have nowhere to turn for help.

1. What does <u>they</u> refer to in the passage?

   a. refugees   b. 15 million people
   c. displaced people   d. asylum seekers

2. Which is the most appropriate for the blank?

   a. Nevertheless   b. Furthermore   c. As a result   d. On the other hand

Unit 4 Too Many College Graduates

Vocabulary Practice

A Write each word or phrase next to its correct definition. Then write its meaning in your language.

| minimum wage | loan | hover | vocational | arise |
| unemployment rate | welder | stable | compound | labor |

1. reliable and unchanging _____ _____
2. to begin to happen; to occur _____ _____
3. a person who works joining metal _____ _____
4. to stay near or hang around something _____ _____
5. money that people borrow and repay later _____ _____
6. relating to working, usually with the hands _____ _____
7. to add to something bad or to make it worse _____ _____
8. relating to skills, training, etc. needed for a particular job _____ _____
9. the number of people in a place who do not have a job _____ _____
10. the lowest amount of money companies must pay their workers _____ _____

B Use the words or phrases from A to complete the sentences. Change the forms if necessary.

1. Allen's leg injury was _____ by his back problems.
2. Many problems in life _____ when you are not being careful enough.
3. Most people take out a large _____ to help them pay for their house.
4. Lawmakers decided to raise the _____ from $7.25 to $9.50 an hour.
5. The daytime temperature is expected to _____ around 35 degrees for the next few days.

8

Writing Practice

C Circle the correct words and translate the sentences into your language.

1. Not everybody needs to get a college degree to (succeed / success) in life.

   ➤ _____

2. The unemployment rate (among / above) young adults hovers at 15 percent or more.

   ➤ _____

3. Germany's youth unemployment rate is only half (that / those) of similarly wealthy nations.

   ➤ _____

4. Millions of people with college degrees have a hard time (to find / finding) suitable jobs.

   ➤ _____

More Reading Comprehension

D Read the passage and answer the questions.

> Many stable, good-paying jobs require college degrees. Yet, when too many young people graduate from college, problems can arise. ⓐ Studies estimate that only 25 percent of jobs today (A) <u>require</u> college degrees. ⓑ This results in millions of young people working in low-salary jobs (B) <u>that</u> often do not require college degrees or even high school diplomas. ⓒ Compounding this issue (C) <u>is</u> the fact that many students graduate from college with large amounts of debt. ⓓ College graduates in America leave school with an average debt of $30,000. Students struggle to pay back their loans while (D) <u>worked</u> in jobs barely paying above the minimum wage.

1. Which is the best place for the sentence?

   > However, in the United States, more than 35 percent of people under the age of 30 are college graduates.

   a. ⓐ b. ⓑ c. ⓒ d. ⓓ

2. Which one is NOT grammatically correct in the passage?

   a. (A) b. (B) c. (C) d. (D)

Unit 4 9

Unit 5 Andy Warhol, Inventor of Pop Art

Vocabulary Practice

A Write each word or phrase next to its correct definition. Then write its meaning in your language.

| attend | in depth | devote | prolific | industrial |
| disorder | churn out | commercial | coal miner | mass-produced |

1. in a detailed way; thoroughly _____ _____
2. concerned with making a profit _____ _____
3. made in large numbers, usually in a factory _____ _____
4. to create a product quickly in large numbers _____ _____
5. to regularly go to a place like a school or church _____ _____
6. a person who removes coal from under the ground _____ _____
7. to use something for a single or special purpose _____ _____
8. a condition of the body or the mind that is not healthy _____ _____
9. describing something related to factories, construction, etc. _____ _____
10. describing someone who has produced many novels, artworks, etc. _____ _____

B Use the words or phrases from A to complete the sentences. Change the forms if necessary.

1. Due to his physical _____, Frank can't play most sports.
2. Roslyn decided to _____ her life to helping children from poor families.
3. Isaac Asimov was a(n) _____ writer, having completed more than 500 books.
4. Sorry, I can't talk now. I have to _____ an important meeting in five minutes.
5. The article explains the problem of global warming _____ with many examples.

Writing Practice

C Circle the correct words and translate the sentences into your language.

1. He spent many days in bed (listened / listening) to the radio.

    ➤ _____

2. Warhol was famous for (not wishing / wishing not) to explain his art in depth.

    ➤ _____

3. The Andy Warhol Museum is the largest museum in the United States (devoted / devoting) to a single artist.

    ➤ _____

4. Warhol remained a prolific artist until his death in 1987, (producing / having produced) over 1,500 works throughout his life.

    ➤ _____

More Reading Comprehension

D Read the passage and answer the questions.

> Warhol took commonly used consumer items, such as Coca-Cola bottles and cans of soup, and created mass-produced images of them. ⓐ He was reselling images of things that (A) was for sale in supermarkets everywhere, (B) presenting these products as they are. ⓑ For instance, he called his prints of soup cans *Campbell's Soup Cans* and his prints of cola bottles *Green Coca-Cola Bottles*. ⓒ His art studio (C) was called the Factory, (D) which was where he constantly churned out his works in the same way that factories produce their products. ⓓ

1. Which is the best place for the sentence?

    > It was there that he made pop art.

    a. ⓐ   b. ⓑ   c. ⓒ   d. ⓓ

2. Which one is NOT grammatically correct in the passage?

    a. (A)   b. (B)   c. (C)   d. (D)

Unit 5 11

Unit 6 What Is Pop Music?

Vocabulary Practice

A Write each word or phrase next to its correct definition. Then write its meaning in your language.

| genre | hook | catchy | aim at | synthesizer |
| tempo | verse | oriented | corporate | top the charts |

1. likeable and memorable _____ _____
2. concerned with or focused on _____ _____
3. to be at the highest position in a list _____ _____
4. related to companies rather than individuals _____ _____
5. a specific section or part of a song, poem, etc. _____ _____
6. to focus on a specific person, group, thing, etc. _____ _____
7. a certain style or type of music, movie, book, etc. _____ _____
8. the speed of a song in terms of beats per minute _____ _____
9. a machine that uses computers to imitate instruments _____ _____
10. the part of a song, story, etc. that gets a person's attention _____ _____

B Use the words or phrases from A to complete the sentences. Change the forms if necessary.

1. This song is so _____. I can't stop singing it!
2. One of my favorite _____ of music is rock and roll.
3. A lot of today's music is made with _____ in music studios.
4. This movie is _____ young adults, but older adults like it, too.
5. An effective way to start your essay is with an interesting _____.

Writing Practice

C Circle the correct words and translate the sentences into your language.

1. They have had a major influence (by / **on**) the development of modern popular music.
   ➤ _____

2. Pop music is defined as any music that is distinct (**from** / for) classical, jazz, and rock music.
   ➤ _____

3. These genres were originally influenced by Western pop groups (**such as** / because of) The Beatles and the Beach Boys.
   ➤ _____

4. Some criticize pop music for being a corporate genre of music, not (**one** / ones) resulting from artistic feelings.
   ➤ _____

More Reading Comprehension

D Read the passage and answer the questions.

> Since the 1960s, pop music has been aimed at teenagers and young adults. ⓐ Most pop songs are professionally produced and medium in tempo and in length, usually around two-and-a-half to four minutes long. ⓑ The main instruments are human voices and synthesizers. Pop songs have good rhythms and simple structures. ⓒ This genre of music usually has a faster tempo than general pop music and is more dance-oriented as a result. Most songs feature a catchy hook followed by verses and a chorus with lyrics that deal with love and relationships. ⓓ Using such a structure, pop music aims to appeal to as many people as possible.

1. Which sentence is NOT needed in the passage?

   a. ⓐ   b. ⓑ   c. ⓒ   d. ⓓ

2. What is the passage mainly about?

   a. the origins of modern pop music   b. regional varieties of pop songs
   c. the common characteristics of pop music   d. the reason why pop music is popular

Unit 6 13

Unit 7 Staple Foods Around the World

Vocabulary Practice

A Write each word next to its correct definition. Then write its meaning in your language.

| protein | staple | via | edible | considerable |
| comprise | temperate | dominant | cultivate | macronutrient |

1. safe for eating _____ _____
2. by means of; through _____ _____
3. to make up something _____ _____
4. fairly large in size or amount _____ _____
5. to grow or raise crops for food _____ _____
6. taking up the largest part; primary _____ _____
7. an important nutrient necessary for good health _____ _____
8. an important nutrient that comes from meat and beans _____ _____
9. used to describe a climate that is not too hot or too cold _____ _____
10. an important food that makes up a large portion of our diets _____ _____

B Use the words from A to complete the sentences. Change the forms if necessary.

1. Soft drinks are _____ almost entirely of water.

2. The United States is _____ in the global entertainment industry.

3. If you want to know if a food is _____, you should check the appearance, smell before tasting it.

4. Today's farmers can _____ huge amounts of food thanks to tractors and other technology.

5. My math homework took a(n) _____ amount of time to complete. Now, I have to go to bed.

Writing Practice

C Circle the correct words and translate the sentences into your language.

1. Over 50,000 edible plant species are known to (**exist** / existing).

    ➤ _____

2. Your diet contains (**considerable** / considerate) amounts of rice, wheat, or corn.

    ➤ _____

3. Staple foods contain three or more macronutrients considered (**essential** / essentially) for health.

    ➤ _____

4. These foods are referred to as staples (although / **because**) they are a dominant portion of many people's diets.

    ➤ _____

More Reading Comprehension

D Read the passage and answer the questions.

> The most produced crop in the world is maize, otherwise known as corn. (A) <u>First grown</u> in Central America over 10,000 years ago, maize is the most widely grown crop in the United States today. China, Brazil, and Mexico also produce large amounts of it. Rice is the main staple in Asia but is (B) <u>widely eaten</u> throughout the world. In fact, it is the main staple food for over half the world's population. Scientists believe it was first cultivated in either Australia or China and was introduced to the West (C) <u>via trade</u>. Rice grows best in warm, wet regions, such as <u>those</u> around the Ganges River and the Mekong River. The third main staple food is wheat, thought (D) <u>to had come</u> from the Fertile Crescent located south of Turkey from Egypt to Iraq. Wheat thrives in areas with temperate climates and is mainly grown in China, India, the United States, and Russia.

1. What does <u>those</u> refer to in the passage?

    a. scientists   b. regions   c. climates   d. amounts

2. Which one is NOT grammatically correct in the passage?

    a. (A)   b. (B)   c. (C)   d. (D)

Unit 7 15

Unit 8 Free-Range Farming

Vocabulary Practice

A Write each word next to its correct definition. Then write its meaning in your language.

| roam | specify | forage | regulate | susceptible |
| humane | livestock | ensure | requirement | slaughterhouse |

1. morally correct; ethical   _____   _____
2. to search an area for food   _____   _____
3. to make sure; to guarantee   _____   _____
4. something that is needed; obligation   _____   _____
5. a place where animals are killed for food   _____   _____
6. to control an activity usually through laws   _____   _____
7. to walk around an area with no particular purpose   _____   _____
8. easily affected or injured by something; vulnerable   _____   _____
9. to outline or establish a set of rules for doing something _____   _____
10. animals that are raised for food, such as cows and chickens _____   _____

B Use the words from A to complete the sentences. Change the forms if necessary.

1. The survivors had to _____ for food in the jungle to survive.
2. The judges _____ the rules of the events for all the competitors.
3. The most _____ way to end an animal's suffering is killing it quickly.
4. In the past, most people raised some _____ for food at their homes.
5. Young children and senior citizens are more _____ to diseases than other people.

Writing Practice

C Circle the correct words and translate the sentences into your language.

1. People are becoming more conscious (with / **of**) eating healthy.
   ▶ _____

2. The result is meat and dairy products that are both (health / **healthier**) and tastier.
   ▶ _____

3. Conventionally raised livestock spend their entire lives (**trapped** / trapping) in tiny cages.
   ▶ _____

4. It refers to a farming system where the animals are allowed (spending / **to spend**) some time outdoors during the daytime to roam.
   ▶ _____

More Reading Comprehension

D Read the passage and answer the questions.

However, critics point out that the term free range, especially in the United States, is vague. ⓐ Also, because free-range animals do not receive antibiotics, they are more susceptible to diseases. ⓑ Often when a free-range animal becomes sick or infected, it is killed rather than being given medication. _____, many free-range animals are killed in the same slaughterhouses that factory-farmed livestock is killed in. ⓒ This calls into question whether free-range farming is really more humane. ⓓ

1. Which is the best place for the sentence?

   > There is no requirement specifying how often or how long the animals must stay outdoors to be labeled as free range.

   a. ⓐ   b. ⓑ   c. ⓒ   d. ⓓ

2. Which is the most appropriate for the blank?

   a. Otherwise   b. Thus   c. Furthermore   d. Yet

Unit 8 17

The Spaceship Cemetery

Vocabulary Practice

A Write each word next to its correct definition. Then write its meaning in your language.

| drag | accuracy | substantial | cemetery | inaccessibility |
| debris | landmass | meticulously | gravitational | decommissioned |

1. any large area of land _____ _____
2. with great care or detail _____ _____
3. to pull something with difficulty _____ _____
4. a place where the dead are buried _____ _____
5. the state of being correct or proper _____ _____
6. the state of not being able to reach _____ _____
7. large in amount or value; considerable _____ _____
8. small pieces that have separated from a larger object _____ _____
9. describing a ship that is no longer being officially used _____ _____
10. relating to gravity, which is the force that causes things to fall toward Earth _____ _____

B Use the words from A to complete the sentences. Change the forms if necessary.

1. Europe and Asia make up the largest _____ in the world.
2. After the car accident, there was a lot of _____ on the street.
3. Make sure to double-check your information to increase its _____.
4. Despite its _____, lots of people eat at this restaurant each day.
5. People can jump higher on the moon because it has less _____ pull.

Writing Practice

C Circle the correct words and translate the sentences into your language.

1. Russia was the first (crashing / **to crash**) a spacecraft there in 1971.
   ➤ _____

2. Since that time, hundreds of rocket boosters have (**crashed** / been crashed) at the site.
   ➤ _____

3. The craft are dragged closer and closer to the surface (**because of** / without) Earth's gravity.
   ➤ _____

4. This spot was chosen (**for** / by) the obvious reason that there is almost no chance of debris crashing into populated areas.
   ➤ _____

More Reading Comprehension

D Read the passage and answer the questions.

> Crashing MIR into the Spaceship Cemetery was a substantial challenge for scientists. Yet, a (A) <u>very</u> greater challenge lies ahead: the future decommissioning of the International Space Station (ISS). Almost four times (B) <u>larger than MIR</u>, the ISS is over 100 meters long and weighs more than 500 tons. It will come crashing down (C) <u>into</u> the Pacific Ocean after <u>it</u> is decommissioned In 2028. Scientists will need to make extensive calculations (D) <u>to ensure</u> that all the debris lands in the water.

1. What does <u>it</u> refer to in the passage?

   a. the debris b. MIR c. the ISS d. the Spaceship Cemetery

2. Which one is NOT grammatically correct in the passage?

   a. (A) b. (B) c. (C) d. (D)

Unit 9 19

Unit 10 Ancient Chinese and Egyptian Astronomy

Vocabulary Practice

A Write each word or phrase next to its correct definition. Then write its meaning in your language.

| catalog | superstitious | precede | align | constellation |
| revere | sophisticated | observatory | burial | infrared light |

1. to come before something   _____ _____
2. to be in a line with something   _____ _____
3. to respect and admire greatly   _____ _____
4. to record information in a list   _____ _____
5. the act of putting a dead body into a grave   _____ _____
6. a place where astronomers observe the sky   _____ _____
7. rays of light that cannot be seen by the eye   _____ _____
8. advanced and including many details or parts   _____ _____
9. a group of stars that appears to form an image   _____ _____
10. relating to a system of belief based on luck or chance   _____ _____

B Use the words or phrases from A to complete the sentences. Change the forms if necessary.

1. Most people have a ceremony prior to a _____.
2. You are _____ if you knock on wood for good luck.
3. One of the most famous _____ is the Big Dipper.
4. Some animals can see _____, even though humans cannot see it.
5. One of the pictures is not _____ with the others. Please straighten it.

20

Writing Practice

C Circle the correct words and translate the sentences into your language.

1. Astronomers (revered / were revered), playing a priestly role in Egyptian society.

   ➤ _____

2. Modern telescopes send an object's light to a computer, which then (forms / form) an image of the planet.

   ➤ _____

3. This was observed as occurring at the time of year (when / where) the sun appears to be farthest north.

   ➤ _____

4. Astronomers were expected to predict the approximate date (which / on which) the Nile River would flood.

   ➤ _____

More Reading Comprehension

D Read the passage and answer the questions.

> Ancient Chinese astronomers were superstitious. **ⓐ** They believed the appearance of a dragon constellation preceded the rainy season. **ⓑ** They worked (A) to map and catalog every observable star. The *Chinese Classic of History* recorded a solar eclipse in 2137 BCE. Later, the Chinese constructed large observatories. **ⓒ** From these, many astronomical (B) phenomenon were recorded. In 613 BCE, Halley's Comet was seen, and in 532 BCE, an exploding star, (C) called a nova, was recorded. **ⓓ** Other events such as sunspots and meteor showers also (D) attracted the attention of Chinese astronomers.

1. Which is the best place for the sentence?

   > *However, they carefully noted what they saw in the sky.*

   a. ⓐ   b. ⓑ   c. ⓒ   d. ⓓ

2. Which one is NOT grammatically correct in the passage?

   a. (A)   b. (B)   c. (C)   d. (D)

Unit 11 Advertising in the Internet Age

Vocabulary Practice

A Write each word or phrase next to its correct definition. Then write its meaning in your language.

| jingle | block | potential | embed | integrate |
| budget | reach | widespread | crucially | banner ad |

1. very much; extremely _____ _____
2. possible or likely to be _____ _____
3. to get someone's attention _____ _____
4. to combine from multiple parts into one _____ _____
5. to insert something into another, larger thing _____ _____
6. to stop or prevent something from happening _____ _____
7. a short, catchy song that is used in an advertisement _____ _____
8. an advertisement that appears at the top of a webpage _____ _____
9. the amount of money expected to be needed to do something _____ _____
10. happening over a wide area or among many people _____ _____

B Use the words or phrases from A to complete the sentences. Change the forms if necessary.

1. You will need to _____ information from the textbook into your essay.

2. Police were placed outside the office to _____ the protestors from entering.

3. The storm is not affecting us now, but it could become a _____ problem later.

4. A good way to _____ young people is by talking about subjects that interest them.

5. Our department's _____ has been reduced this year, so we will have to fire some staff.

Writing Practice

C Circle the correct words and translate the sentences into your language.

1. The Internet allows users (controlling / **to control**) the content they see.

   ➤ _____

2. Along with (seen / **seeing**) posts from your friends, you will often see advertisements.

   ➤ _____

3. Many marketing firms are creating ways to integrate it (**into** / from) a website's content.

   ➤ _____

4. This number is far too low for companies and websites (for making / **to make**) much profit on their advertising.

   ➤ _____

More Reading Comprehension

D Read the passage and answer the questions.

> Currently, over 80 percent of advertising budgets are used for traditional media advertising. ⓐ This includes ads for radio, newspapers, magazines, and television. ⓑ Companies spend over $100 billion globally each year on Internet advertising, and this figure continues to rise. ⓒ In the early days of the Internet, most ads were in the form of pop ups and banner ads. ⓓ Today, browsers usually block pop ups automatically, and most users _____ banner ads. One research group found that these ads had a click-through rate of just 0.06 percent.

1. Which is the best place for the sentence?

   > *Even so, Internet advertising is crucially important for most companies.*

   a. ⓐ   b. ⓑ   c. ⓒ   d. ⓓ

2. Which is the most appropriate for the blank?

   a. ignore   b. check   c. prefer   d. develop

Unit 11 23

Unit 12 Customized Online Ads

Vocabulary Practice

A Write each word or phrase next to its correct definition. Then write its meaning in your language.

| relevant | packet | disable | make for | drawback |
| violation | contend | customize | preference | opt out of |

1. related to the topic _____ _____
2. a problem or disadvantage _____ _____
3. to choose not to do something _____ _____
4. the act of breaking a rule or right _____ _____
5. what a person usually likes better _____ _____
6. computer information in small amounts _____ _____
7. to allow or cause something to happen _____ _____
8. to argue or believe something to be true _____ _____
9. to change something to how you want it to be _____ _____
10. to stop something from working; to deactivate _____ _____

B Use the words or phrases from A to complete the sentences. Change the forms if necessary.

1. To _____ the alarm, you need to enter the PIN first.
2. Driving too fast is a _____ that is punishable with a ticket.
3. To _____ receiving these emails, just click the box below.
4. You can _____ your T-shirt so that it says whatever you want.
5. Jessica _____ that her mom gave her too much housework to do.

Writing Practice

C Circle the correct words and translate the sentences into your language.

1. Customized ads (do come / does come) with some drawbacks.
   ▶ _____

2. Internet companies contend that customized ads (make up / make for) a better browsing experience.
   ▶ _____

3. Cookies are text files that can only (read / be read) by the websites that send them to your computer.
   ▶ _____

4. Internet companies claim they do not share their users' personal information (to / with) advertising companies.
   ▶ _____

More Reading Comprehension

D Read the passage and answer the questions.

> Many websites display customized advertisements based on many factors. These include the websites you have visited, the key words you have searched for, and your location. ⓐ Using this information, Internet companies are able to show ads that are more relevant to each user. ⓑ For those concerned about privacy, there are some solutions. ⓒ For example, suppose someone often visits cooking websites and watches instructional cooking videos online. ⓓ This person will likely see ads for cooking products. _____, businesses, ranging from international corporations to locally owned shops, can earn more money.

1. Which sentence is NOT needed in the passage?

   a. ⓐ 　　　b. ⓑ 　　　c. ⓒ 　　　d. ⓓ

2. Which is the most appropriate for the blank?

   a. On the contrary 　b. Nevertheless 　c. At once 　d. At the same time

Unit 12 25

Unit 13 — Why Can't Ostriches Fly?

Vocabulary Practice

A Write each word next to its correct definition. Then write its meaning in your language.

beak	rump	stimulus	predator	opponent
outclass	feathery	attribute	formidable	breastbone

1. the chest bone _____ _____
2. like feathers; very light _____ _____
3. to be superior to others _____ _____
4. the rear part of an animal's body _____ _____
5. quite a lot in size, power, or amount _____ _____
6. a feature or characteristic of something _____ _____
7. an animal that kills other animals for food _____ _____
8. the hard pointed part covering a bird's mouth _____ _____
9. something that causes a change or reaction _____ _____
10. someone who you compete against in a competition _____ _____

B Use the words from A to complete the sentences. Change the forms if necessary.

1. Sylvia's loud laugh is her most distinctive _____.
2. Black bears are a major _____ of white-tailed deer.
3. Anthony _____ all the other competitors by finishing first in the race.
4. Babies will move their eyes towards a(n) _____ such as their mother's voice.
5. Climbing to the top of this mountain has been a more _____ challenge than I expected.

Writing Practice

C Circle the correct words and translate the sentences into your language.

1. (No / Not) other bird can run as fast as an ostrich.
   ▶ _____

2. Ostriches are equipped with the biggest eyeballs (in / of) any bird.
   ▶ _____

3. Without this stimulus, these birds gradually lost their ability to (fly / flying).
   ▶ _____

4. (Because / Although) ostriches are superior to other birds in many ways, they will never be able to take to the skies.
   ▶ _____

More Reading Comprehension

D Read the passage and answer the questions.

> Even so, ostriches cannot fly because of their physical attributes. Flying birds have a keel, which is the bone that is attached to the muscles that move a bird's wings, but ostriches lack one. Birds that can fly also have a rounded breastbone while the ostrich's breastbone is flat. _____, the wings of an ostrich are short and incapable of flight. Like other flightless birds, ostriches also tend to have more feathers than <u>those</u> that can fly.

1. Which is the most appropriate for the blank?

   a. Furthermore   b. Nevertheless   c. Thus   d. For instance

2. What does <u>those</u> refer to in the passage?

   a. feathers   b. ostriches   c. birds   d. wings

Unit 13 27

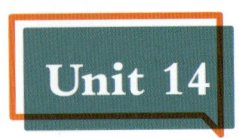

The Swimming Nose

Vocabulary Practice

A Write each word next to its correct definition. Then write its meaning in your language.

| fin | grip | tendency | submerge | intimidating |
| adept | durable | undertake | synthetically | misconception |

1. strong and long lasting _____ _____
2. frightening or threatening _____ _____
3. the usual way of doing something _____ _____
4. a mistaken belief about something _____ _____
5. to go below the surface of water _____ _____
6. artificially; by using manmade means _____ _____
7. the act of holding something very tightly _____ _____
8. to begin doing a long or difficult activity _____ _____
9. good at doing something quite difficult _____ _____
10. a thin, triangular part on a fish, which helps it to swim _____ _____

B Use the words from A to complete the sentences. Change the forms if necessary.

1. Road surfaces need to last many years, so they must be _____.
2. One _____ about Americans is that they always eat junk food.
3. Scientists are working to grow meat _____ to replace meat raised on farms.
4. Although moving to a new school can be _____, it can also be a lot of fun.
5. I took a good _____ of my father's hand as I walked down the aisle of the church.

Writing Practice

C Circle the correct words and translate the sentences into your language.

1. They have discovered that sharks have (astonished / astonishing) senses.

   ➤ _____

2. Sharks are responsible (for / of) the deaths of an average of six humans each year.

   ➤ _____

3. People think of a shark (as / like) a blue triangular fin cutting through the ocean surface.

   ➤ _____

4. The 400-million-year-old animal is (high / highly) adept at detecting the nearness of other fish.

   ➤ _____

More Reading Comprehension

D Read the passage and answer the questions.

> _____ their image as a scary predator, thousands of sharks are hunted and killed each year for products that can (A) be produced from their skins. Sharkskin is (B) covered with tiny teeth-like objects called denticles. In Japan and Germany, sharkskin was used to make sword handles because its nonslip surface provided a good grip. Sharkskin was also used (C) as sandpaper to smooth out rough surfaces and is used as a leather to make durable shoes. Sharks are also hunted for their liver oil, (D) that is rich in vitamin A, even though a method has been devised synthetically to produce it.

1. Which is the most appropriate for the blank?

   a. Due to   b. In addition to   c. Regardless of   d. Contrary to

2. Which one is NOT grammatically correct in the passage?

   a. (A)   b. (B)   c. (C)   d. (D)

Unit 15 The First Modern Olympics

Vocabulary Practice

A Write each word or phrase next to its correct definition. Then write its meaning in your language.

| revival | step in | overrun | proclaim | aristocrat |
| approve | delegate | recognizable | reinvigorate | countryman |

1. easy to know; noticeable _____ _____
2. to defeat quickly and easily _____ _____
3. to say or state something officially _____ _____
4. a person from the same country as you _____ _____
5. to think that something is good or acceptable _____ _____
6. to give energy and power back to something _____ _____
7. a person born into a rich, upper-class family _____ _____
8. a representative for a country or business at an event _____ _____
9. the act of bringing something back to a previous condition _____ _____
10. to become involved in a difficult situation to provide help _____ _____

B Use the words or phrases from A to complete the sentences. Change the forms if necessary.

1. His army was able to _____ the armies from most other countries.
2. I was surprised to meet a fellow _____ on the other side of the world.
3. The city is trying to _____ downtown by encouraging new businesses to open.
4. In Europe, _____ were the second highest members of society below royalty.
5. Harry tried to let his son solve the problem by himself, but he had to _____ to help out.

Writing Practice

C Circle the correct words and translate the sentences into your language.

1. As an adult, he thought that the world needed to stop (fighting / to fight) wars.

    ▶ _____

2. Competitors had little financial support (from / for) their national governments.

    ▶ _____

3. France suffered defeat and occupation (although / when) German soldiers invaded.

    ▶ _____

4. This was the same route run by a Greek soldier, (which / who) was delivering news of a Greek victory.

    ▶ _____

More Reading Comprehension

D Read the passage and answer the questions.

> In 1894, Coubertin's campaign for a revived Olympics (A) was approved by 79 delegates from nine countries. ⓐ It was the French aristocrat and educator's dream (B) to hold the event in its ancient home of Athens. ⓑ The first modern Olympics almost got moved to Budapest, Hungary, until a Greek businessman (C) called George Averoff stepped in and contributed a million drachmas. ⓒ With this money, the ancient Panathenaic Stadium, originally built in 330 BCE, could be reconstructed. ⓓ It was there on April 6, 1896 (D) which King George I of Greece declared, "I hereby proclaim the opening of the First International Olympic Games at Athens."

1. Which is the best place for the sentence?

    > *There were, however, funding problems.*

    a. ⓐ 　　　b. ⓑ 　　　c. ⓒ 　　　d. ⓓ

2. Which one is NOT grammatically correct in the passage?

    a. (A) 　　　b. (B) 　　　c. (C) 　　　d. (D)

Unit 16 Calendar Systems of the World

Vocabulary Practice

A Write each word or phrase next to its correct definition. Then write its meaning in your language.

| lunar | adopt | in line with | leap year | exception |
| solar | calculate | straightforward | modification | auspicious |

1. relating to the sun   _____   _____
2. relating to the moon   _____   _____
3. a change or adjustment   _____   _____
4. to begin using something   _____   _____
5. simple to understand; direct _____   _____
6. in the same position as something else _____ _____
7. a year that has an extra day or extra month _____ _____
8. to find out a number, answer, etc. by using mathematics _____ _____
9. indicating or suggesting that future success is likely _____ _____
10. something that is different from normal or expected _____ _____

B Use the words or phrases from A to complete the sentences. Change the forms if necessary.

1. After 2016, the next _____ is 2020.
2. Could you explain this concept to me in a(n) _____ manner?
3. He decided to _____ a more traditional approach to the problem.
4. I want to make a small _____ to our travel schedule so we leave later.
5. One of the most _____ occasions in people's lives is graduating from college.

32

Writing Practice

C Circle the correct words and translate the sentences into your language.

1. One of the oldest known calendars (is / are) the Mayan calendar.

    ▸ _____

2. In East Asia, the Chinese lunar calendar remains (influential / influentially).

    ▸ _____

3. It is used to choose auspicious days to have weddings, move home, or (starting / start) a business.

    ▸ _____

4. (When / While) no longer the official calendar, the Chinese calendar is still used in China to celebrate traditional holidays.

    ▸ _____

More Reading Comprehension

D Read the passage and answer the questions.

> The most (A) widely used calendar in the world today is the Gregorian calendar. It was introduced in the 16th century (B) by Pope Gregory XIII as a modification to the Julian calendar. Each year in the Gregorian calendar is divided into 12 months of 365 days. The exception is the leap year, which (C) have 366 days and occurs every four years. _____ is added to keep the date of the calendar more (D) in line with the movement of the sun. In the late 19th century, most countries adopted it for international business purposes.

1. Which is the most appropriate for the blank?

    a. This extra month   b. The first day
    c. The additional year   d. This extra day

2. Which one is NOT grammatically correct in the passage?

    a. (A)   b. (B)   c. (C)   d. (D)

Reading Voyage 3

PLUS

Reading Voyage is an eleven-level reading series divided into four stages: Starter, Basic, Plus, and Expert. The series is designed for high-beginner to low-advanced EFL students who want to enhance their reading abilities. The passages cover a wide range of topics that enable learners to expand their background knowledge. The various exercises will allow students to develop their reading comprehension, critical thinking, and vocabulary skills.

Key Features

- Appealing and informative texts covering a variety of topics
- Vocabulary in Context to help identify word definitions and synonyms
- Comprehension questions to help identify main ideas and details
- Reading Skill and Summary to help students analyze key concepts
- Language Focus to enable students to learn key grammar structures

Components

Student Book / Workbook

Download Resources at www.darakwon.co.kr :

MP3 files / Answer Key / Translations / Vocabulary lists

Scan this QR Code for MP3 files

Reading Voyage Series: PLUS

260-280 words

280-300 words

300-320 words